Praise for *The Neur*

"*The Neuroscience of Taro*t brilliantly bridges scientific rigor and mystical intuition. This unique and important book demystifies the complexities of neuroscience, presenting them in a manner accessible to all readers, whether they have a background in science or not. Ramakrishnan's masterful approach intertwines practical exercises with insightful narratives, offering a transformative journey into understanding the brain's role in intuition, psychism, and divination. It's an indispensable resource that stands out for its ability to show how our cognitive processes and spiritual practices intertwine in both an understandable and engaging manner."

—MAT AURYN, author of *The Psychic Art of Tarot* and *Psychic Witch*

"An essential addition to the tarot reader's library. Learn how your brain works when engaging in psychic predictions or neuroforecasting. Dr. Ramakrishnan masterfully applies neuroscience concepts to the art of divination and reading tarot. This book offers invaluable insights into how a scientist might observe, hypothesize, and investigate the realm of intuition. Truly one of the most exciting and groundbreaking books to come out of the tarot world in a long while."

—BENEBELL WEN, author of *Holistic Tarot*

"*The Neuroscience of Tarot* beautifully bridges brain, mind, and body for an integral, practical approach to tapping into our innate wisdom. This is exactly the kind of work we need to synthesize modern biology with ancient intuitive traditions and practices."

—MONA SOBHANI, PHD, author of *Proof of Spiritual Phenomena: A Neuroscientist's Discovery of the Ineffable Mysteries of the Universe*

THE
NEUROSCIENCE
OF TAROT

About the Author

Siddharth Ramakrishnan, PhD, is a neuroscientist and educator with over twenty years of experience. His work explores the developing brains of animals and how brain hormones are influenced by the environment. With a PhD from the University of Illinois and postdoctoral research from UCLA and Columbia University, he is a professor of biology and the chair of neuroscience at the University of Puget Sound. He has been awarded the prestigious National Science Foundation CAREER award, as well as the W. M. Keck Foundation award to establish an initiative for neuroculture at his institution. Aside from these, he has published in numerous scientific publications including *Nature*, *Neurotoxicology*, *AI & Society*, and *Experimental Biology*.

A fellow of the UCLA Art | Sci Center, his collaborations with artists have led to exhibitions and documentaries that blend the worlds of art and science, highlighting topics like *Hox genes*, animal umwelts, and biomimicry. An avid tarot reader for the last twenty years, he explores the intersections of science, art, and mysticism. This led him to design and create the Neuro Tarot deck, which is inspired by the major arcana of tarot but infused with neuroscience concepts. A lifelong educator, he has also created courses for diviners to explore how the brain moves from imagery to intuition and also how to design your own tarot decks. He has been featured as a keynote speaker at the Northwest Tarot Symposium 2023 and as a featured speaker at NWTS 2022. Siddharth also was invited to host a workshop by Mary K. Greer at the Masters of Tarot Workshop at the Omega Institute in summer 2023.

You can find more about him at www.brainmystic.com.

THE
NEUROSCIENCE
OF **TAROT**

FROM IMAGERY
TO INTUITION TO
PREDICTION

SIDDHARTH RAMAKRISHNAN PHD

LLEWELLYN

WOODBURY, MINNESOTA

FIRST EDITION
First Printing, 2024

Book design by Christine Ha
Cover design by Shira Atakpu
Interior illustrations by the Llewellyn Art Department
Tarot Original 1909 Deck © 2021 with art created by Pamela Colman Smith and Arthur Edward
    Waite. Used with permission of LoScarabeo.

Llewellyn Publications is a registered trademark of Llewellyn Worldwide Ltd.

Library of Congress Cataloging-in-Publication Data (Pending)
ISBN: 978-0-7387-7736-8

Llewellyn Worldwide Ltd. does not participate in, endorse, or have any authority or responsibility concerning private business transactions between our authors and the public.

All mail addressed to the author is forwarded but the publisher cannot, unless specifically instructed by the author, give out an address or phone number.

Any internet references contained in this work are current at publication time, but the publisher cannot guarantee that a specific location will continue to be maintained. Please refer to the publisher's website for links to authors' websites and other sources.

Llewellyn Publications
A Division of Llewellyn Worldwide Ltd.
2143 Wooddale Drive
Woodbury, MN 55125-2989
www.llewellyn.com

Printed in China

सरस्वति नमस्तुभ्यं वरदे कामरूपिणि।
विद्यारम्भं करिष्यामि सिद्धिर्भवतु मे सदा ॥

Sarasvati Namastubhyam Varade Kaama-Ruupinni |
Vidyaarambham Karissyaami Siddhir-Bhavatu Me Sadaa | |

—

CONTENTS

JOURNAL EXERCISES

BRAIN ILLUSTRATIONS

IMAGES

FOREWORD

This divination book is the only one of its kind, and so I feel honored to write the foreword.

I've been teaching tarot for over fifty years, many of those in a university and in a liberal arts college. I've also studied psychology and psychic development and was part of the San Francisco Human Potential Movement of the 1970s and '80s. In addition, I learned from the best in the divinatory field by attending hundreds of tarot and astrology conferences.

In 2022 I met Siddharth Ramakrishnan, a scientist and tarot reader who offers a perspective on and knowledge of neuroscience so often overlooked in the divinatory fields; it is something that I have struggled to understand on my own.

The materials here will be invaluable to any advanced card reader, astrologer, or diviner who wants to practice their art and skill at a truly professional level. It can also be a boon to beginning and intermediate enthusiasts who wish to have confidence in their intuition and insight when reading for themselves or others.

People historically and cross-culturally turn to divinatory methods in times of stress and confusion and when our normal ways and expectations of life are not operating as usual. They want new options, fresh perspectives, and alternatives outside their normal patterns of activity. One's natural tendency to avoid risk is countered by the benefits of expanded horizons and the use of imagination and creativity in perceiving new possibilities, which is bolstered by the belief in some kind of internal or external guidance or purpose. In order for this to happen, people have to step outside the constraints of rational thinking and behavior based on society's rules and traditions.

Siddharth offers ways to tune your brain, improve intuitive processes, recognize emotions, and listen to your body—the mechanisms we use to make intuitive leaps and resonate with a querent.

I can't help but go back to an analogy with a revolutionary book that came out in 1969 called *How to Keep Your Volkswagen Alive*, also known as *The Volkswagen Repair Book*. By demystifying car maintenance, it empowered individuals to do their own vehicle upkeep, fostering a DIY ethos. During a time of countercultural movements, the book aligned with the desire for self-sufficiency and independence, symbolizing a shift away from reliance on traditional authorities. This newfound ability to understand and maintain one's "folk-vehicle" resonated with a broader cultural shift toward individual empowerment and self-reliance during the 1970s and '80s.

Siddharth's book gives us a similar look at what goes on in this vehicle we call the body when interpreting a divinatory card, spread, astrology chart, and the like. Through the deceptively easy exercises, self-evaluation tools, and explanations of how perception works, we gain clarity about where an intuition comes from. Even more importantly, it empowers us to improve our use of intuition and the related empathy and psychic abilities that are our underappreciated navigation tools through life.

Over the past half century, there has been a tremendous amount of research into what scientists call intuition. One of the major findings is that intuition, in general, is only right about half the time.

Intuition is a fifty-fifty proposition that is clouded by our biases, prejudices, beliefs, expectations, and opinions. It needs to be developed like any other ability. Intuition, even with only 50 percent accuracy, gives us several benefits and opportunities. Among the things mentioned previously, there is its speed, accompanied by a sense of rightness that inspires us to take action. Science has shown that intuitive abilities, insights, and the predictions that spring from the unconscious interactions of body, mind, and emotions can be greatly improved.

I define intuition as the instantaneous firing of previously established neural pathways in response to sensory input. This input interacts with our emotions, prior knowledge, and experiences. Intuition is triggered by our environment through our physical senses. By contrast, psychic experiences are delivered through what are known as the "clair" senses; they are "extrasensory" and then interpreted via our personal associations. How we experience the world is based on how the brain and body predict what may happen given our past experiences. How we interact with the world around us alters how we perceive the world.

Diviners, especially tarot readers, are inevitably drawn to images and seek to understand what the images signify. Siddharth understands this and provides us with copious images of the interior of our bodily vehicle that will sensitize us to its functioning. Meanwhile, in a reading, we externally follow a terrain mapped out by the cards in a spread brought to life by the narrative or story we tell of the journey that includes predictive scenarios of what will come next.

In addition to the processes we go through within ourselves, tarot readers also tend to be naturally gifted in what is called social cognition. This perception can be developed to a greater extent through the exercises Siddharth gives here as he takes you through the processes a querent typically undergoes when at the receiving end of a reading. For instance, in most decks, a dog is pictured at the heels of the Fool. A person's own associations with and experience of dogs will color both a reader's perceptions and emotions as well as those of a querent that may or may not accord with the standard interpretation of the Fool or of a dog. Here you see how bias, for instance by someone who has been attacked by a dog, can deeply influence their reaction to such an image.

In 1781 the author of a multivolume scientific encyclopedia sought to demonstrate how the wisdom of ancient Egypt lay hidden in the modern world. In volume 8 of *Le Monde Primitif*, Antoine Court de Gébelin tells how he happened upon a card game he recognized from childhood although it was no longer played in Paris. He cast his eyes on the World card and "at once I recognized the allegory … with all that is known of Egyptian ideas." He stated how it took him less than a quarter hour to explain to those present the allegories contained in the twenty-two trumps, observing that their frivolous form "made them capable of triumphing over the ages." It was essentially this flash of instantaneous intuition and, as he clarified, "not imagination" that allowed him to recognize "all at once" the entire allegory portrayed. Antoine Court de Gébelin was absolutely wrong. Tarot was not from Egypt, but his intuition still served to launch a public interest in an occult and divinatory tarot.

The majority of people who become tarot enthusiasts have had a first or early reading for someone else when, despite knowing little about the cards, they blew the mind of the querent at the relevance of what was being said. People are either hooked or spooked off by this.

One of the initial things you hear when learning tarot is to trust the very first thought or image that comes to mind. Our critical faculties plus doubt shut down intuition. It is essential for insight and inspiration to not be hindered by these secondary mental processes. Intuition works astonishingly well for perceiving a *meaningful* significance between an image and the question or concern asked.

This book goes even further than that via Siddharth's explanations, experiences, and mindful awarenesses that fine-tune intuition to an incredible degree. For instance, whether you have memorized tarot card meanings or studied the significance of the symbols on the cards, intuition plays a huge part in helping you identify the big picture pattern revealed by the interplay of cards drawn, the spread positions, the question, and the querent (whether yourself or another).

Siddharth provides us with the missing piece in the training of diviners— a piece that takes us into relatively uncharted territory by combining the mechanics of what's going on inside the body-brain regarding our intuition with the intent of supercharging that intuition. Through the exercises, Siddharth gives us the training and practices that will allow both our skills and the physical mechanism behind them to improve markedly.

Every field of endeavor or job has its training. As someone who has spent over fifty-five years immersed in tarot, I find that to read the cards most consistently and effectively we need to bypass the critical and limiting restraints of the rational mind. But we additionally need to eliminate our knee-jerk biases, opinions, and attitudes in order to be fully present to other ways of knowing. We can become much more aligned with our inner knowing through the kinds of understanding and training found in this book.

May this book and the recommended activities in it serve you well.

—Mary K. Greer,
author of *21 Ways to Read a Tarot Card*
December 2023

INTRODUCTION

The story of this book perhaps begins on a cold spring day in Seattle when I wandered around the neighborhood of Ballard, a coffee run leading me into a mysterious basement labyrinth housing the Seattle Metaphysical Library. Or perhaps the story begins much earlier, almost two decades earlier, when I was studying snail brains, hiding the side of myself with a penchant for astrological musings. But somewhere in 2001, my sister gave me a set of tarot cards and so began mutual readings between the discussions of *Gilmore Girls* episodes and latest experimental and love woes. But wherever the story begins, it leads me to this point, where I am trying to understand and then explain how we use our brain for intuitive insight and divination.

So, how did a neuroscientist happen to dive into the world of tarot? In some ways, I had no control over it. My father is a surgeon and my mother an artist; so I have forever been juggling art and science. On top of that, having grown up in India, the realm of astrology, magic, and myth was never separated from everyday life. Even for small events, we consulted charts and picked a good hour or day. Surgeries were planned for appropriate hours. Temples were sanctuaries where faith and prayer were part of the routine. At school, meditation and mantras were prescribed curricula, as was yoga, so the mysticism was never anathema. I was a kid who loved making up stories based on images that popped up from the jumble of mosaic tiles on our floors. Thus intertwined, my science training was never in conflict with art or the Divine.

When I moved to Chicago, I discovered tarot. I was intrigued by the few readings that I got, and about a year in, my sister, who was also a connoisseur, sent me my first tarot deck. We then started reading for each other and do so to this day. From there, word got around, and I started reading for friends and family and for myself when I needed clarity. But here on the Western shores, within

PhD programs and science settings, my mystic bent was sent into the closet and became more of an add-on to my own quirky personality.

Around 2008, I started collaborating with artists and began to dive back into my artistic side. Public exhibitions, installations, and talks led me to truly embrace that I was not just a scientist but an artist as well. Around 2018, I felt that my spiritual journey was stagnating, and I needed to learn more. This was a period where I felt alone, despite having friends, family, and loved ones near and afar. The constant gaze and touch of the electronic medium also gave me pause, and I wanted to get back into the tangible production of art. For some reason, I wanted to connect that with my own spiritual journey, and I started using tarot cards to get some clarifications on decisions and paths. It was then that I envisioned designing Neuro Tarot cards—inspired by the major arcana of the tarot but infused with neuroscience concepts. Initially I thought I needed to collaborate with an artist to render the cards, but my few attempts failed. Then it hit me—who else had both the science background and the tarot knowledge but me. I needed some breakthrough for me to accept that my own artistic abilities could be enough.

Thus began an almost yearlong journey that involved studying the cards, their symbolism, and their meaning and using that research to then layer neuroscience concepts on them. As I moved forward creating and sketching my deck of Neuro Tarot cards, I started to think about what went on in my brain as I created them. Where were all these combinations and correspondences coming from? Where were these links between the meaning in the tarot and the neuroscience concepts? And as I worked on them, signs started popping up around me—things that could not be ignored. Despite having lived in Seattle for over eight years, I had never heard of the Seattle Metaphysical Library. And then, just when I was working on this deck, I just happened to see a sign for this place on a random coffee run. How bizarre, and yet how appropriate!

Perusing books through that library gave me pause, as a lot of information and research on tarot was done by academic scholars. Maybe I needed that validation to ensure that I was not all kooky. But whatever it was, I dove deep into the research behind how we use images and imagery, move into intuitive guesses, and gain insight from them. On the one hand, my Neuro Tarot deck was being rendered and published, and on the other hand, I started learning more about the mechanisms by which we use information from the world around us to become diviners. And it was/is so exciting! Who knew our brains had such predictive capabilities? Who knew we could leap from point A to point C with a few cues? Who knew neuroforecasting was something actually being studied?

My art fed my curiosity, that fed my tarot research, and that led me down a rabbit hole into the world of tarot, archetypes, and symbols and into the brain. As a lifelong educator, I truly believe that there is a wonder within us and outside, and it needs to be shared widely. That is my main motivation for this book: to spread my love for neuroscience and how it connects with something magical—divination.

What Is Divination?

Divination can mean many things to many people. Some may define it with regards to foretelling or using auguries or omens to interpret events. For the purposes of this book, we will consider divination to be about having extraordinary intuition or unusual insight. I wrote this book researching a lot of scientific articles and books, and at the moment of this writing, there is not much evidence regarding supernatural phenomena. This does not by itself disprove the existence of such phenomena. Toward the end of the book, I do talk about the ability of the human brain to predict events and how it may relate to forecasting.

As scientists we observe, hypothesize, and investigate. Our experiments rely on tools and technology of the moment, and our observations and interpretations rely on our sense organs, how we perceive the world, and the limitations of those instruments. At this moment in time, we do not have tools to truly investigate some elements of the "supernatural." Maybe we have to develop more sensors to examine energy fields or auras. We also have to come up with a more clear, precise definition of consciousness and how to measure it. There is so much work to be done. Given these limitations, I have restricted this book to what can be learned from current literature and how to become better with the tools that we have: tarot cards, astrological charts, and our brains!

What Is Neuroscience?

Neuroscience is the study of neurons, how they connect together, and their function to elicit behaviors. The field of neuroscience stretches beyond just the brain and goes into the control of the body, the function of the mind, and also how we interact with each other. Neuroscience is a bridge between biology and psychology, providing the physical framework for many of the abstract concepts that psychology raises. Historically neuroscience was a reductive science, as one needed to understand the building blocks of how things are made in order to understand how they function. But as the field has matured, and with new technological tools (especially in genetics and neuroimaging), neuroscience has started to explore and tackle larger questions related to the mind, social cognition, consciousness, meditation, animal-human interactions, and more. It is an exciting time to be in the field, as we have a chance to ask more esoteric questions and try to find answers.

In the context of this book, think of neuroscience as not just the brain but also the body and the mind. Think of it also as not just an individual perception but in terms of how it relates to empathy and perception of the other, of the self, and of the self in relation to the other. In this book, we will talk about both the building blocks and what emerges from them.

Why the Neuroscience of Divination?

All of us are intuitive and act on intuition. Many of the split-second decisions and choices we make are based on this. We humans are also highly visual creatures who take in a lot of ideas from the images we see around us. Our brain is also an entity that needs to constantly categorize, label, and make sense of what we see. When I look up at clouds, I see shapes—dragons or ships or lions. Stargazers have been connecting stars into patterns of constellations across centuries and cultures. Perhaps you have seen images peeking out of tree branches or bark or even in lush grass. Everywhere we look, there are patterns and stories waiting to be told of these configurations. Many of our intuitive decisions are made by unconscious observations of such patterns in the world. Our brain quickly takes in a bunch of information, forms a narrative around it, and tells you, "Hey! This is what we need to do right now." And some of us willingly seek out signs that help us clarify what is in front of us. Perhaps you use this intuition to invest in stocks, download a song from some random list, pick the best turn on a long walk, or to answer questions on an exam. Maybe you make life decisions based on these gut checks. Should I buy this house? Is this pet for me? Is this my forever person? Every one of us uses the process of intuition. In the case of divination, we use imagery from tarot cards or patterns from astrological charts to spark the intuitive path and bring it to the surface. These cards and charts give us a peek into our brains to help form a conduit between our conscious and unconscious thoughts.

To that end, who is this book for? We all rely on intuition in our everyday lives, in our professions, hobbies, and businesses. We will all benefit from peeling back the curtain on how the brain looks at patterns and symbols around us and helps us make leaps of faith, thereby moving forward. The metaphors and examples used in this book are geared toward someone who uses the symbols and imagery of tarot cards. However, you can easily extend the imagery to oracle cards or patterns in astrological charts. But even if you do not dabble in such esoteric forms, you can think of how you use patterns around you (maybe body cues, colors, signs from the universe, data trends—whatever they may be) to make gut-check decisions and predict outcomes. If you want to know what makes you intuitive and get better at it, this book is for you.

Dissecting the Divination Process

So, why try to understand how the divination process works? As thinkers, many of us are inherently curious about how all of this works. For diviners, the main instrument in interpreting any signs from cards, charts, or other auguries is the brain. In effect, the big questions are "How does my brain do that?" and "Why did I think of that?" The hope is that this book will be able to answer those questions. Aside from the curiosity-driven inquiry that pushes us to ask these questions, this book also allows us to dwell on the process of using our intuition and gain insight from it, thereby helping us become better at recognizing signs, overcoming biases, and removing blocks. Some of us may get stuck on certain themes and interpretations, and sometimes our first instinctual intuitive associations may also be wrong. Understanding the processes that help shape these phenomena can help us recognize these biases and mistakes and correct them.

The other aspect is that many of us, while looking at imagery, tend to focus on certain details; most of us are trained to do so based on our childhood experiences, the environment we grew up in, and what we are taught to look out for. This adds a cultural layer to what one notices on top of the innate observer within each of us. This is also why no two diviners will give you the exact same interpretation of signs. Even those who are looking at the same cards or charts are observing entirely different cues and using them to arrive at certain conclusions based on their own past associations. Knowing your own process of divining or interpreting will help you learn to recognize patterns in your readings, any crutches that you use, or themes that emerge constantly. From there, what makes us have those intuitive gut feelings that allow us to interpret what we see? Can we then reflect on these intuitions, and gain insight to become better at making these choices moving forward? Along the way, I give you exercises and examples that can help you hone your craft, become better at probing your brain, and thereby improve your divination techniques.

While it is easy to dwell on the brain as the instrument of divination, we tend to forget that the body keeps the score and our emotions are encoded in the body. Every divination reading is a walk through the miasma of emotions, choices that affect our mental states—and every reading is also constantly filtered through the emotional state of both the reader and the questioner. We will wade through how the brain processes emotions. In many cases, divination is not an isolated event but is transactional between a diviner and a querent. It is interesting to see how we respond to others, how we recognize their energies and then use that in our readings. It is also exciting to see how one receives such information and what is heard in a reading. We will try to understand how divination is more than what the diviner sees or says and the importance of what you think and what the others are thinking. Finally, we will delve into the interesting new field of neuroforecasting and try to glean how our brains are predictive machines and how we can tap into them.

I hope this will be an exciting journey and a quest for discovery into yourself, a way into that magnificent tool of yours—your brain. While I am primarily using the visual imagery of tarot cards as my entry point, you can think of any interpretive divination tool—oracle cards, astrological charts, or others—using the neural circuits in similar ways. After all, each of these techniques are but tools that provide information that you have to analyze, interpret, and gain insight from. I hope you enjoy the journey and share your experiences.

How this Book Is Organized

Even as young kids, we take things apart to look at the little bits and pieces, to figure out what goes where and how it all fits together. It is much later in life that we start to think in terms of abstractions and philosophy. Most of the field of neuroscience is also this way; to understand the brain, we dissect it out, look at individual cells, and see how they all connect with each other, adding more and more information that harmonizes with each other until we build up to concepts such as consciousness. As a scientist trying to understand how we see the world around us, how we follow "signs of the universe" and make leaps of faith, I have tried to use a similar path—first deconstruct and look at the elements, then slowly build them up again to see how it all leads us into the divining brain.

One note: Throughout this book I have used the terms *diviner* and *reader* to signify the person who is interpreting tarot or oracle cards, reading the astrological chart, or using other divination tools. I have used the terms *querent* and *questioner* to signify the person who puts forth the question. Traditionally this person will approach the diviner and state a problem that needs clarity. Then the diviner will read some auguries to answer the question at hand. It could also be that you just do readings for yourself. In this case, you will be both the querent and the diviner. As mentioned before, you do not have to engage in tarot, oracles, or astrology to make use of this book. It is all about seeing patterns in images and how we use them to interpret our own behaviors, emotions, and choices. Substitute an image or a symbol for a tarot card, and you are good to go!

In this book, we start by discussing how we process images and how we see them with our mind's eye. We will explore what leads us to label images or words with meanings and why we associate pictures, words, and sounds with emotional scenes and behavioral choices. This is something we do constantly as visual creatures, breaking down what we see and rebuilding it in our brain but at the same time coding it, labeling it, and making it meaningful by adding colorful associations and emotional tags. This allows us to experience the world not just as it is but as we picture it in our mind. The way each person sees the world is unique, and therefore, how you interpret the signs that you "see" in images or charts will be different from what I would see in them. The metaphors that you use to describe them would be different from the ones that I would use. We will discuss how our brains make these unique associations and how we can learn to recognize them.

As animals, we have instincts. We can anticipate events and prepare for them. But humans are also intuitive; many of us take actions based on an underlying gut feeling that makes the choice or decision "just right." This is our intuition. Even though we don't know why we make a particular choice, we are sure that it is the right one. Diviners, be they tarot or oracle readers or astrologers, rely on this sense of intuition. Neuroscience studies intuitive abilities using game players who are able to guess moves of opponents, athletes who just know where balls will land, doctors who rely on intuitive diagnoses, and many others. In chapter 2, we will discuss what the neural basis of intuition is and how we can become better at using it. Further, we will delve into the processes behind insight, the "Aha" moment when you realize how you came to a particular conclusion. Having insight and reflecting on it helps us to become better at using our intuition and thereby become better at our divination.

Intuition relies a lot on body responses. "Having a gut check" and "making a choice that makes our heart feel lighter" are not just turns of phrases but actual responses that the body has that the brain interprets as emotions. Aside from our external senses, which allow us to perceive the outside world through smell, taste, hearing, touch, and sight, we also have a host of internal sensors that constantly send signals from inside our body to the brain. These are then collected and packaged into emotions. A lot of our intuition relies not just on brain interpretations but on body responses. We discuss these cues as we all rely on them, consciously or unconsciously. This allows us to paint a more detailed picture of events. Chapter 3 will teach you to recognize these emotional cues and better tune in to them, allowing you to use those bodily signs in your intuitive processes as well.

In most cases, divination is a two-way street. A questioner approaches a diviner to interpret their astrological chart or use tarot decks or other divination tools to answer questions. This results in a transaction between two individuals and a whole host of mental processes. The diviner takes in not just the question of the querent but also unconsciously processes their body language, their tone, the nature of the words used, and their mental state. This delves into the realm of social cognition, which we as humans constantly use to engage with people around us. We are constantly trying to predict the behaviors of others with minimal information. And this is a process used in divination as well. During this, the diviner uses metaphors that come up in their brain to create a narrative that is then divulged to the querent. How they make sense of this story narrated to them is another interesting step in this process. The querent hears what they hear. This is dependent on their attention, their intention, and their mental state—all of which filter the story that the diviner says. We will try to parse out this two-fold processing and what emerges from this transaction.

Animals, including humans, need to constantly anticipate events and plan ahead. This can be instant to instant, seasonal, or over much longer periods. Somehow our brains have this capacity to anticipate and prepare for the next step. This is the predictive brain. We have built in correction mechanisms that learn from past mistakes and then predict the next possible steps. Scientists have long studied these phenomena. But more recently, some have delved into the realm of forecasting. Can a group of people, unaware, predict events or situations that are six months ahead? Is there any basis to the idea of precognition? While the primary focus of this book is not on using divination as a means of prognostication, I wanted to explore the current science behind such ideas.

The book is interspersed with lots of journal exercises that will help hone your intuitive abilities and better listen to your body and process the emotions of others. In many ways, it is to bring awareness to the different steps we use in the divination process. To this end, we conclude by exploring some spreads of tarot cards, a fun way for you to engage and exercise your intuitive capabilities while also learning about the different brain parts that you use in this process.

Anatomy of the Brain

We will talk about different brain regions, and while a primer in neuroanatomy is not necessary to get through this book, it might be useful to get a few landmarks of your head.

Use your hands to feel the different parts of your head. Run your hands across your forehead. Behind it sits the forebrain, or the frontal lobe, your seat for executive reasoning (Illustration 1, blue). Pass your fingers over your eyebrows and feel the bones of the eye orbits beneath. Behind this is the main area where your current mental states are being recorded, the orbitofrontal cortex. Slowly move your hands toward your temples—the place that you massage for headaches or sometimes press when you want to remember things. Beneath is the brain area recording time (the temporal lobe), where you are able to remember things, place them in sequence, or even categorize them (Illustration 1, green). This is also the place for empathy. Go behind your ears and locate the base of your skull above the neck. This is the main visual area, or the occipital lobe (Illustration 1, yellow). Move your hands to the top of your head, in line with your ears. This is where you will find the parietal lobe (Illustration 1, pink), which we will talk about during object recognition and also in discussion of the self and the other. Come down to the nape of your neck. There lies the brain stem, which controls all your unconscious functions, such as breathing, sleep-wake cycles, and biorhythms (Illustration 1, gray).

Sometimes brain anatomy uses language that becomes difficult to parse. But if you know the individual words, it usually becomes easy to navigate. Imagine scanning your head from one ear to the other. The parts of the brain toward the outside are called lateral. The parts of the brain toward your midline (in line with your nose and third eye) are called medial. Next scan your head from the crown (top) to your neck (bottom). The areas of the brain closer to the top (the sahasrara, or crown chakra) are called dorsal. Those closer to the base of your skull are called ventral. Finally, scan your head from your nose to your back. Areas of the brain closest to your nose are anterior. Those closest to the back are posterior.

I have tried to avoid using too much jargon. But every so often, I do use scientific terms to describe brain parts. For those who love such nerd talk, you can dive in deeper. For the others, feel free to just let it slide. Refer back to this first figure from time to time. At the beginning of each new chapter, there is an illustration of brain pathways that will help you navigate the main structures discussed in that chapter. There is also an empty brain illustration following the glossary in case you want to doodle on it.

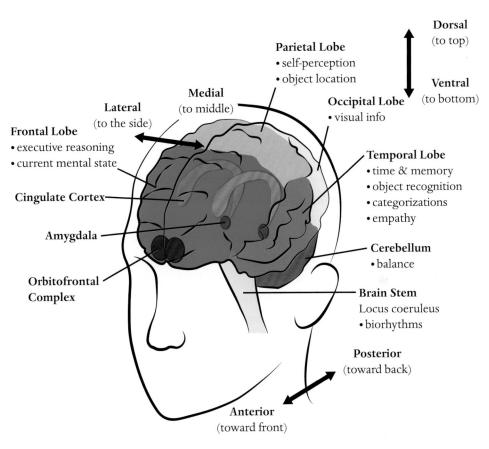

Illustration 1: Basic Brain Anatomy Landmarks

How to Use this Book

Use this book as a tool to understand how your brain works during simple tasks, such as seeing and recognizing objects, to more complex associations and cognitive processes such as intuition and insight. You can use it as a way to improve your observation skills and intuitive abilities; journal exercises under each section allow you to become better at not just understanding concepts but using the skills. You will also learn to listen more to the body and attune yourself to emotional perception through your embodied self. The hope is that some of these exercises will make you more aware of your entirety, allowing you to recognize why you make certain observations, why you feel a certain way, and why this colors your story or narrative during a divination process.

During divination you are responding to nonverbal cues, tone, and the "feeling" of the other. I hope that you are in a place to receive these mostly unconscious cues that feed into our insight and learn from them so that you get better at reading them or understanding what makes you go down a particular rabbit hole in the brain.

I suggest to use this book as a mindfulness exercise. The hope is for you to become more aware of your brain and body and how you use them in your practice or intuitive meanderings. When you are asked to intentionally notice, take the time and space to do so and become aware of that twinge in your body or that interpretation in your brain, and then let it go. Of course you can psychoanalyze yourself and dwell on those little details but that could interrupt the flow of a reading. So, you can do that later. As you work through these exercises, notice, make a note, and move on. It's like when you meditate and you are asked to take the breath through one nostril and then let it out through the other, feeling the breath going in and out—just notice, make a note, and let go.

I anticipate that this book will function better as a workbook or a journal that you spend time working through, so I don't anticipate you finishing it in one sitting. Instead, dwell on journal exercises and ruminate on them before moving forward. And of course, I would suggest you revisit the exercises again after a few weeks or months and compare notes to what you wrote down before. This might be the most beneficial for your own intuitive practice.

When you work through the exercises, try to go through them step-by-step. This will allow you to intentionally slow down and think about brain processes. Before you start, I would recommend having a journal by your side for jotting notes. Have your favorite divination tool handy. Many of the exercises use tarot imagery from a Rider-Waite-Smith-based tarot deck. But you can substitute that with astrological chart metaphors, oracle cards, everyday objects, or even random images. If these do not appeal to you, I would suggest having a group of everyday objects or magazines/websites with random pictures available to walk through some of the visualization and intuition exercises. Finally, some exercises do ask you to phone a friend or many friends to compare notes, so having your favorite social media site on tap may come in handy as well. Do remember that there is no right or wrong answer. All the reflections and journaling are for you and discovering yourself. Have fun with them!

The book can also serve as a neuroscience resource for you to understand your own brain when you are wading through the process of divining. A glossary, bibliography, and an index have been provided, which you can use to delve deeper into the brain. There are also brain maps and other charts that you can use in your own readings so that when you feel stuck, you can recognize where in the process the stagnation occurs.

I hope learning more about yourself and your inner gears will be a fun and fruitful process—and you become a more magical being.

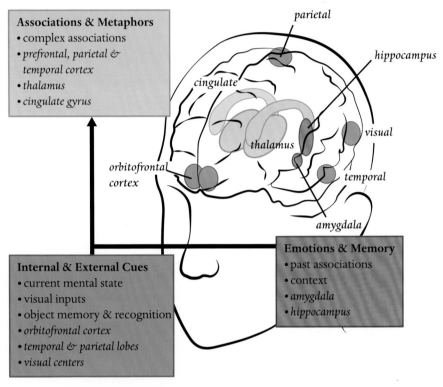

Associations & Metaphors
- complex associations
- *prefrontal, parietal & temporal cortex*
- *thalamus*
- *cingulate gyrus*

parietal

hippocampus

cingulate

visual

thalamus

orbitofrontal
cortex

temporal

amygdala

Internal & External Cues
- current mental state
- visual inputs
- object memory & recognition
- *orbitofrontal cortex*
- *temporal & parietal lobes*
- *visual centers*

Emotions & Memory
- past associations
- context
- *amygdala*
- *hippocampus*

Illustration 2: Anatomy of Imagery and Associations

We process sight with our visual centers in the back of the head and then recognize objects using other areas (temporal and parietal lobes). This, along with your current state of mind in the front of the brain (green), is then tagged with emotions and memory in the amygdala and hippocampus (red). Both of these are then put together to form associations and metaphors, leading to stories and narratives (blue). The cingulate cortex and the thalamus, alongside the prefrontal cortex, are essential for forming meaningful ideas from mere pictures.

CHAPTER 1

FROM IMAGE TO IMAGERY TO IMAGINATION

While humans have a myriad of senses, we have come to rely on visual inputs for navigating the world. Not only do these serve as ways for us to interact with everyday objects but they also serve as conduits for making up themes and scenes within which we immerse ourselves. We also have the capacity to replay some of these in our heads, even with our eyes closed. This chapter will walk us through the rich sense of visual imagery and how we see with our mind's eye. It will shine a light on how you parse out information from pictures and attach meanings to them.

Capturing the World in the Blink of an Eye

I pull out a card from my tarot deck. It is the Three of Wands (Image 1), with a person looking at the horizon as ships wander away. Rays of sunshine creep out from the clouds, and maybe the person smiles or cries; we are not purview to that. As I look further at the card, I think of journeys taken and those not taken, of someone looking wistfully at the past or the future. None of these narratives are written on the picture, but yet my mind wonders at the picture and wanders, making up stories. Why? What is the point of these stories and how am I making them up? To really understand this, we need to deep dive into how we really see images and how that leads to interpretations. The card, after all, is just a small rectangular piece of paper with some markings on it.

Image 1: Just Look at the Card: Three of Wands

My eyes are open when I take in the image of the card. The little details move from my lens to the back of my eye, the retina. It is sort of like a pinhole camera, and the world is captured onto this. The lights, patterns, and colors excite cells on the retina and make them fire up or simmer down, sending pulses of electricity that streak forth, screaming, "Ooh! Incoming information!" These pulses race from the eye into the center of the brain, which rearranges the images, categorizing left and right, up and down. It's like a picture captured on your camera or a shadow projected on a screen, and you are not even aware that you have seen something. From deep inside the brain, the signal fire races to the back of the head (the occipital lobe, or your visual center), where all the visual images are first gathered. Here is where the full picture is put together again, bit by bit, with edges and colors, a replica of what you see out there. Even now, it is but a projected copy, with no meaning or concept attached, but if at this moment, I peeked at the back of your head in the visual areas, I may be able to recognize what you are seeing (Illustration 2).

Making Sense of the World

The brain needs to make sense of the world. That is the only way we can function. Anything we take in has to be categorized and labeled, else we will not be able to understand or make use of it. Even things that you think you don't notice, you do, and the brain may then choose to ignore them. Most of our young years, we learn how to codify things around us—we watch, we listen, we smell, and we make connections that add names, ideas, and meanings to things. Later we call on these labels to make sense when we navigate the world. Each of us is unique, as we each have our own labels. Even if I say the word *turquoise*, a specific type of blue, the color you think of may be much different than mine.

Imagine wearing a headband with bunny ears. As you look back on the Three of Wands, the image now rendered in your head, the fire spreads from the back of the head (the visual centers) to two parts of the brain. The top of your head, where the bunny ears are (Illustration 1, the parietal lobe), helps us recognize movement, allowing us to catch objects and sense their speed. To the side, where your imaginary bunny ear headbands end and just in front of your ears (Illustration 1, the temporal lobe), is where the object is finally recognized based on past labels. The temporal and parietal lobes add value and tags to what you have seen. The parietal lobe starts by placing the image in context, allowing you to recognize its movement, its positionality, its distance, while the temporal lobe adds meaning and labels from your memory storehouse, finally allowing you to recognize the object. This is where you begin to see a flower for what it is, adding "words" to label what you see, adding context based on what you have learned so far. These brain regions are where the long lines on the Three of Wands blossom into wands with budding flowers, waves are seen on the ocean, the ships gain movement, and the yellow streaks now become rays of glorious sunshine. The brain is rendering the sketch with meaning—all in a fraction of a second.

Journal Exercise 1
NOTICING

A lot of observation and perception is just taking the time to notice what is around us. This exercise will help you slow down your perception process and figure out when you start layering simple observations with more nuanced labeling. Use your journal or this book to note down your observations.

You will need: Your journal, a writing utensil, and a deck of tarot cards

1. Look around you. Notice objects in your surroundings. Write down observations about what you see.
2. Now, try to notice things without attributing values/names/ feelings to them.
3. Write down your observations. Describe objects without labels or judgments (e.g., a table could be a flat surface with four legs).
4. Look at a random tarot card. Try to notice just the lines and edges. Bring the card toward you or move it away, focusing in and out. Write down your observations.
5. As you observe, is there a point at which the card becomes more than just a jumble of lines and colors? Note when the card becomes meaningful for you.

Contemplate: What minimum image details do you need to find meaning in a card?

The Ghost in the Brain

As I write this, the tarot card I picked, the Three of Wands, is no longer in front of my eyes, and yet, even if I close my eyelids, I can still see it, or at least bits and pieces of the image in my head. It is present in my brain as though a remnant or a haunting of the image. This is what is called seeing with our "mind's eye," and it can be done with no external input. For some of us, this imagery is vivid, rich with colors, azure seas with golden rays and pink blossoms. For others (like me), the image is not as vivid but still clear enough to recognize what it is. For some of you, there may be no images at all; perhaps you will see just words or colors when you try to picture something with your mind's eye. Scientists have found that seeing with your mind's eye evokes the same excitement in visual centers of your brain as seeing the actual picture, albeit in a much more subdued fashion.[1] You can think of it as the ghost of an image (Illustration 3).

This mental imagery does not need to be just of something you have just seen. I can ask you to close your eyes and picture a table or a sunset. For some

---

1. Pearson et al., "Mental Imagery," 590–602.

of us, a kitchen table would emerge, perhaps with chairs around it and flowers, while others may picture a sturdy desk that needs varnish. Still others may only "see" a rectangle with four posts, the minimal needs for identifying a table. The extent of vivid visualization runs the gamut from people with photographic mind's eyes to those with none! It would be good for you to identify how strong your mental visualization is. This is not to say that if you lack the "visual" visualization you will not be good at divination. You may be quite adept at using words or language in your brain to conjure up scenarios, or perhaps acoustic or smell signals evoke more vivid memories in your brain. Delving into how you conjure up your own mind's eye will help you home in on your strengths, allowing you to become better at recognizing and interpreting signals.

Seeing with Eyes Open | **"Seeing" with the Mind's Eye**

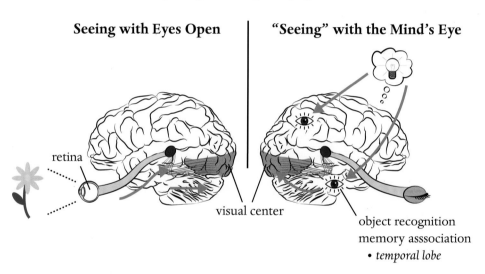

retina

visual center

object recognition
memory asssociation
• *temporal lobe*

Illustration 3: Seeing with the Mind's Eye

Even with the eyes closed, one can still "picture" images in their head. Mental imagery still evokes responses in the visual centers, even though no actual input is coming in from the eyes.

Mental imagery of cards or readings becomes important, especially if some of them evoke strong interpretations that we become fixated on—and find hard to move away from. For example, when I first started in tarot, I used to dread the Devil card. I had only heard negative tropes about the card and was also going through my own suppressed emotions, so when the card appeared in a reading, it would immediately cause a sinking feeling in me. Even when the diviner provided a positive spin on the interpretation of the Devil, I could not move past my own associations with the symbolism and negative connotations. The mental imagery this card evoked in my head was already biasing my outlook on what it meant in a reading.

This is not to say you should ignore all negative meanings or interpretations—but it is important to check if you gravitate toward one particular meaning for a card each time despite all other signals and contexts or if you are not open to new ways of "looking" at the images because of some trauma or deep pain associated with some of the symbols. These negative associations could also arouse emotional reactions that occlude other information. This could lead to biases, not recognizing that we are repeating past loops of emotions, and not interpreting what the card means in the current situation. If you recognize that you are stuck in an image-interpretation loop, it may be useful to perform some cleansing visualizations in order to clear the brain and make the ghosts less potent.

Journal Exercise 2
VISUAL CLEANSING

Sometimes we need to wiggle away from an image or a thought. This exercise will help you clear your sensory inputs.

You will need: Four herbs/spices, coffee beans, some cups, a writing utensil, and your journal; a deck of cards, a blank piece of paper, a writing utensil, and your journal. You can also use a timer if you like.

Clearing Your Olfactory Sense
Part 1: Warm-Up
Try not to take breaks as you move through these steps.

1. Lay out four herbs/spices in front of you. Smell them one after the other. Write down in your journal what you smell after each herb/spice.

Part 2: Using Coffee Beans as an Olfactory Cleanser

1. Using the same herbs/spices as part 1, smell one of them. Again, write down in the journal what you smell.
2. Before moving on to the next herb/spice, smell some coffee beans.
3. Repeat 1 and 2 for all herbs.

Part 3: Reflection

1. Compare your notes from part 1 with your notes from part 2.
2. Observe similarities and differences.
3. Note any changes in how you described what you smelled. Did the cleansing help?

Clearing Your Visual Sense

Part 1: Warm-Up

1. Pick a card.
2. Look at the image for two minutes, using a timer if you would like.
3. Close your eyes and visualize the image of the card in your head for a minute.
4. After a minute, open your eyes and write down your mental image of the card in your journal.
5. Compare what you wrote down with the image in the card.

Take a five-to-ten-minute break between part 1 and part 2.

Part 2: Ramping Up

Try not to take breaks as you move through part 2.

1. Pick four cards. Keep them closed, or face down.
2. Open one card. Observe for two minutes.
3. Close your eyes and picture it in your head for a minute.
4. Open your eyes and write your mental image of the card in your journal.

5. Repeat steps 2 through 4 for the remaining cards.
6. Lay out all four cards and look at them.
7. Compare what you see at the end with your prior mental imagery observations.

Take a break between part 2 and part 3 (maybe even an hour or a day).

Part 3: Using Blank Paper as a Visual Cleanser
1. Pick the same four cards used in part 2. Keep them closed.
2. Open one card. Observe for two minutes.
3. Close your eyes and picture it in your head for a minute.
4. Open your eyes and write your mental image of the card in your journal.
5. Look at the blank piece of paper for one minute.
6. Close your eyes and visualize the blank sheet in your head for one minute.
7. Repeat steps 2 through 6 for the remaining cards.
8. Lay out all four cards and look at them.
9. Compare what you see with your mental imagery observations.

Part 4: Reflection
1. Compare your notes from part 2 with your notes from part 3.
2. Observe similarities and differences.
3. Note any changes to your descriptions. Did the cleansing help?
4. On a different day, repeat part 3 of visual cleansing, but instead of a blank piece of paper, use white noise on the TV or a blank screen.
5. Again, compare notes and reflect.

Contemplate: How much are your thoughts and imagination influenced by what you see?

Worlds within Worlds

We live in a world, but actually, we live in multiple perceptual worlds defined by other creatures and individuals we share spaces with. This concept is called the *umwelt*, or surrounding worlds. My experience of my surroundings is entirely dependent on my sensory organs. How I perceive the world—how I see, smell, taste, and hear it—is very different from an ant that can see infrared radiations or the bee that can see vivid hues of ultraviolet and polarized light. When you look outside and see some flowers, you may notice the green grass, the blue skies, and the reds, pinks, and yellows. For a bee, the same scene is shifted, and they can see contrasting planes of lights and shadows, intense differences within the whorls of the flowers, and distances measured in dance movements. For a dog, this scenario can be layered with traces of smell, bringing in a rich history of animals that have visited the location over the last three days.

But such differences in perception do not just extend across species. What scientists are now discovering is that cultural upbringing and early childhood experiences change what humans notice and observe.[2] All that you have smelled, tasted, and interpreted before is poured into one cauldron to give you the recipe for noticing things and finding meanings and associations. For example, each time I described the Three of Wands, I waxed on about the ships, the ocean, and the rays of sunshine. Perhaps you noted instead the pleats on the person's robe, the movement in their hair, which rod they were leaning on, or the serpentine vermilion sash across the body. We all notice different things from these images / portents and then interpret them in our own way (which we will get to in the next chapter). Thus, it is your world, and it has a meaning of its own for you.

The art of reading or interpreting any pattern is to take in as much information as we can and evoke our intuition. One way to become better at "seeing" all the details is to exercise our observer skills. Try to overcome your learned behaviors and notice new things about the cards next time. The more you practice this, the better you will become. This will add to the rich associative knowledge you build up with the cards, adding to your metaphors and symbols. So, can you become better at visualizations? The answer seems to be yes; you can exercise these brain circuits just like you exercise muscles. When you learn to

---

2. Nisbett and Masuda, "Culture and Point of View," 11163–70; Kitayama and Salvador, "Culture Embrained," 841–54.

throw a ball, you repeat it over and over again to physically improve your performance, which is called perceptual learning. Similarly, you can "imagine" tasks or events to improve the performance without actually doing the task. Many athletes use this to add to their winning formula. They visualize how they will perform a play again and again prior to the actual game. Many watch videos of themselves and their opponents and picture how their feet, hands, and muscles will move under different scenarios. Some even visualize capturing the trophy as a part of their training regimen.

Such visualization tasks are also used in physical therapy and are the basis of all visualization tools that we employ. There is evidence that when you picture an apple in your mind's eye, you literally "see" an apple in your head. It is a bit faded compared to a regular apple, but it activates the same parts of the brain that seeing an apple would.[3] Similarly, if you close your eyes and picture someone shining a light on them, your pupils will actually constrict—a physiological response to an imagined situation. This is the power of mental imagery and why we need to keep exercising it. In reductionist neuroscience, structure-function relationships are considered very important. But the hierarchy is always structure leading to function. In ayurveda and yoga, there is a greater emphasis on function to form, where the modified functionality leads to altered form. This leads to a more holistic medical approach, where tackling the issues with the body begins with targeting the needed function and not the broken form. A lot of yoga therapy involves asking the mind to picture how the body will behave and then using that to gain functionality. So, all of us have the capability to become better at such visualizations, which gives seeing with your mind's eye greater clarity and purpose.

3. Pearson et al., "Mental Imagery," 590–602.

VISUAL AWARENESS

This exercise helps you recognize steps in the perceptual process. It will give you an idea of when you start adding new meanings to things around you based on memory recall and language.

You will need: Your journal, a writing utensil, and a deck of tarot cards

Part 1: Just Describe
1. Pick a card.
2. Observe the card.
3. In your journal, describe what you see in the image with no additional interpretations or metaphors.
4. Write down how easy or hard it was to just observe the image without racing to find meaning in it.

Part 2: Delving Further into a Card
1. Pick a card.
2. Observe the card.
3. Write down what you see. Include details about location, movement, time, depth, etc. that you notice in the card.
4. Look at the card again. Write down which details in the image prompted descriptors in step 3 (e.g., What makes you say the ships are moving or that he is looking backward? What makes you determine the gender of the person, etc.).

Part 3: Situational Awareness
1. For the next day, carry your journal with you.
2. Note down each time you become aware of an object around you.
3. Note down when you recognize or locate something.
4. Observe what senses you used for becoming aware of objects around you.

Contemplate: What makes even two-dimensional images evoke stories in your head? Why are tarot cards so evocative for you? Do you have a favorite deck? If so, why is it your favorite?

Journal Exercise 4
VIVID VISUALIZATION

Different people have different abilities to recall things with their mind's eye. Some folks have photographic memories and vividness that involves colors and shapes. Others just know they are thinking of things but cannot picture them accurately in their mind. Some may rely more on words, smells, or sounds that pop up when thinking of these things. Some of us may be better at "seeing" faces in our heads as opposed to landscapes, while others may notice details more than others. The following exercise (modified from Marks) will make you aware of what you notice and what you can picture in your mind's eye.[4]

There are no "right" or "wrong" answers to these prompts. Describe as best as you can each of these scenes. If you can picture nothing in your head or just words appear, just write that down. For each prompt, spend a few minutes with your eyes closed, and then a few minutes journaling.

You will need: Your journal, a writing utensil, and a deck of tarot cards

Part 1: Seeing with the Mind's Eye
1. Close your eyes and imagine a friend or a person close to you for a few minutes.
2. Open your eyes and write down the details of the image in your mind's eye. You can describe your mental picture of their face, expressions, body posture, clothes, etc.

---

4. Marks, "Visual Imagery Differences," 17–24.

3. Pick a tarot card from your deck. Then close your eyes and picture the card with your mind's eye for a few minutes.

4. Open your eyes and write down the details of the image in your mind's eye. You can describe your mental picture of any figures in the card, their facial expressions, movement, colors, etc. Describe the background of the card. Describe the foreground.

5. Close your eyes and imagine a sunset or a sunrise for a few minutes.

6. Open your eyes and write down the details of the image in your mind's eye. You can describe your mental picture of objects such as sun rays, clouds, landscape details, colors, etc.

7. Close your eyes and think about a scene from a movie or a show that you recently saw for a few minutes.

8. Open your eyes and write down the details of the image in your mind's eye.

Part 2: Reflection

Based on the descriptions you just wrote down, reflect on your mental imagery. If you like, you can compare notes of your visualizations with those of friends and see how they are similar or different.

1. Images in my head are _____ (vivid/vague/neither vivid nor vague).

2. In this exercise, I had more descriptions of _____ (people/objects).

3. I tended to focus more on the _____ (foreground/background).

4. My mental images were mostly _____ (in color/black and white/no idea).

5. My mental images were mostly _____ (pictures/words/other).

6. I tended to notice movement _____ (a lot/a little/not at all).

7. I visualized real world people better than tarot cards. (Yes!/No!/Sort of the same.)

RETRAINING VISUAL AWARENESS

Sometimes we get stuck noticing only certain aspects of an image or a chart. We then tend to ignore other details—sometimes creating biases. This exercise will help you retrain your brain to remove some of these hardened observations.

You will need: Your journal, a writing utensil, and a deck of tarot cards

Part 1: Intention to Notice
1. Pick several tarot cards (three to five) on day one.
2. Look at one card for a minute.
3. Write down five things you notice about the image.
4. Repeat steps 2 and 3 for all the cards you picked.
5. On the next day, look at the same cards from step 1.
6. Write down one new thing you notice about each of the cards.

Part 2: Tracking Your Eye
1. Pick a card.
2. Write down what part of the image your eye is first drawn toward.
3. On the next day, examine the same card.
4. Deliberately look at a different part of the picture than step 1.
5. Write down your observations and think about these questions. Was there a reason your eye was drawn to certain patterns on day 1? Was it difficult or easy to deliberately look at other parts of the image? Did the image look different to you between days 1 and 2?

Contemplate: Prior to a reading, use the above exercises by picking just one card. Write down one new thing you observe. Deliberately look at a part of the image beyond the first focus. See how it alters your perception of the cards.

The Brain Is Not a Computer

For all the comparisons and metaphors used in everyday life, our brain is not a computer. And more and more scientists are discovering that we are also not equal in our observations and what our eyes are drawn to. Depending on how you were raised and what patterns, questions, and symbols you were taught with, your observational skills—and the parts of the brain you use to process them—may be entirely different. For example, when counting numbers, Asians use the areas of the brain that control movement, and people from the West use the verbal areas of the brain. This is because of the way math is taught at a young age—with characters or the abacus in Asia (involving a lot of movement) and verbal tables in Western society.[5] These kinds of differences also extend to visual observations—what does one notice on the first instance?

Let me draw three tarot cards (the Magician, Knight of Wands, and Page of Pentacles). Even if you don't use tarot, look at these cards (Image 2). Just concentrate on how you think they are related. What patterns do you notice among the images? What is common and how can you group two of the cards together?

Image 2: Finding Relationships: The Magician,
Knight of Wands, and Page of Pentacles

To me, the first two cards (the Magician and Knight of Wands) go together, as they represent action, movement, and agency, while the Page follows. But someone else may say that the Magician and Page are both "rooted" with their feet on

---

5. Tang et al., "Arithmetic Processing in the Brain," 10775–80.

the ground, while the Knight is off with his legs in the sky. You may have noticed the hills and the wide landscapes in the latter two cards and grouped them together, seeing them as the world offering its resources as opposed to the internal/self-centered approach of the Magician. Perhaps the colors of the cards are what stand out for you. How you group these images together, how you form relations between the cards, is dependent on how your brain processes images. What we "observe" or see is very, very different depending on our cultural upbringing. Scientists notice such differences even in six-year-olds from different countries.[6] These are not good observations or bad observations—just different observations. This also makes it interesting, as your individual perspective, angle, and hence divination is unique, making room for all of us in this space.

Journal Exercise 6
MAKING ASSOCIATIONS

This exercise will help you understand how you form associations between different objects or symbols. Awareness of this will help you better comprehend how you use the symbology in front of you (and notice any that you may have missed). Comparing your ideation with friends' allows you to distinguish your process from that of others and identify your own uniqueness and biases. While you move through these questions, ignore card meanings. Just look at the pictures and their details.

You will need: Your deck, your journal, a writing utensil, and some friends

Part 1: Finding Connections
1. Shuffle the deck and pick three cards.
2. Try to ignore the meanings of the cards, and just look at the images. If you were to group two of the cards together, how would you do so?

---

6. Köster et al., "Visual Attention in 5-Year-Olds."

3. Write down the reason for your grouping in your journal.

4. Send some friends the same three card images and ask them to group two of the pictures. Ask them to write down the reason for their grouping.

5. Compare notes on how you all grouped the images and your reasonings.

Part 2: Details

Image 3: Your Mental Imagery: Five of Wands

1. Observe the Five of Wands (Image 3) for ten seconds.

2. Close your eyes and picture the image in your head.

3. Without looking at the card, open your eyes and write down all the things you saw in your mental image.

4. Look at the actual card again.

5. Compare what you wrote down with the card.

6. Make note of the things that you noticed and what you missed.

7. Highlight any details that you added to your mental image that were not in actual picture.

Part 3: Drawing from Memory

1. Draw a city scene or write five words to describe a city.

2. Draw a landscape or nature scene or write five words to describe a landscape or nature scene.

3. Ask a few friends to do steps 1 and 2.
4. Compare notes. Write down similarities and differences.
5. Ask them why they chose specific details or words. Share your own.

Part 4: Reflection

Fill in the blanks based on your observations in parts 1 through 3.

1. I find relationships between images using _____.
2. I focus on _____ details when I picture scenes in my head.
3. I miss out on _____ details when I picture scenes in my head.
4. When I look at a picture and later see it in my mind's eye, they are the same. (True! False! Somewhere in between.)
5. When I picture an image in my mind, I have added details that did not exist before. (True! False! Sometimes.)

Contemplate: How do your memory and associations affect your divination process?

The Karmic Connection

To many people, karma is the product of lives past. Some say it is all the positive and negative actions in previous lives that have accumulated to serve as credits and merits for this one. This is one way to talk about destiny and predestined futures. Another way to view karma is to think of it as all the events in your life that have led you to this point—this moment where you are making a choice, getting a reading, or deciding something. It has got everything to do with your current state—your nature, culture, upbringing, emotions, and actions that have led you to this particular moment in space and time. I like this notion of karma, as it provides one with more agency and choice, offering people choices in front of them and allowing them to gain clarity of what could be affected by their decisions.

This is reflective of what happens in a divination reading. Neither the querent nor the reader is distanced from their past, their current emotional states, or their surroundings. All their experiences, biases, desires, and fears are pertinent for how the lay of the land is interpreted. What things you notice, what images and words pop up in your head—these are not static entities frozen in time but fluid, dynamic, and changeable, like your own brain circuits. There may be countless things that you notice and become aware of, but there are even more countless things that you notice but are unaware of that the brain tucks away for another day. The art of becoming a better reader is to reflect on these unconscious bits and bobs and sort them out upon reflection.

A Layer Cake of Metaphors in the Brain

Our lives are full of sounds, smells, tastes, and images that let us interact with the world but also wander into stories and portals. You don't have to have cards or astrological charts to see patterns and themes around your life. But such items serve as powerful tools that can jolt some ideas out of our unconscious mind and bubble them up to the realm of consciousness in order for us to gain clarity or become more aware of their existence. How we interpret these signs or patterns around us is tied, as we said before, to our internal emotional states and our own experiences and nature. This is because when our brains take up information, it automatically classifies it with relevant meanings from the past and adds emotional valence to it, annotating it with its own words. This is called an association (Illustration 2).

A table could be a kitchen table, a worktable, or a dining table. The images that each of those ideas evoke could be very different for each of us. Based on your past, a kitchen table could evoke either fondness or distress. If it evokes fondness, based on your current mood, this affection could be one of wistful nostalgia or of loneliness. We could layer adjective upon adjective based on numerous scenarios.

Symbols and metaphors abound in the tarot landscape. In fact, for the attuned observer, these are scattered all around our world. Shapes in clouds or clusters on mosaic tiles to patterns in garments or burn marks on toast could all serve as symbols. But where do these ideas emerge from, and how do we attribute images and words with such metaphors? How do we add valence to them, making a picture more than just a picture, making it something that has meaning and allegory?

Let us start with an example:

Image 4: Forming Metaphors

What do you see when you look at this image (Image 4)? A different question may be: What do you "feel" when you look at it?

Take a few minutes to contemplate the image. Write your thoughts down in your journal.

To me, it is a full table filled with fresh food; a lot of love and care has gone into the preparation. The image also fills me with a sense of anticipation, as though the moment I have been waiting for is about to happen but I still need to wait with bated breath.

This image is not a tarot or oracle card nor a mathematical astrological chart—yet it is filled with metaphors that your brain has come up with. There is no explanation in the picture, no words, no cues—yet we are able to fill in the blanks. This is how your mental imagery connects with the other areas of your brain to result in associations and invoke new imagery. For this, we depend on our current internal states (from the prefrontal cortex) and our current emotional states (from the amygdala) as well as the image information from the visual centers, the object recognition areas (Illustration 2, green). This is coupled with past memories and emotions associated with similar objects coming from the hippocampus and the amygdala (Illustration 2, red). These are then layered and textured by other parts of the brain and finally synthesized with the cingulate cortex (Illustration 2, blue).

We use and are manipulated by such associative images every day through advertisements, labels, and movies. These associations result in an internal movie that the brain constantly projects based on the layer cake that you bake inside the association. Images we see are broken apart, and the individual pieces, such as colors, edges, and patterns, become the flour, salt, and baking soda that is baked into a sponge in your visual centers. From there, the sponge is infused with fillings and flavor with the meanings added in the temporal and parietal lobes. We then layer this with fruits and decorations that personalize the cake, adding new meanings and emotions to it. Finally, when we eat the cake, we take in all these layers, the flavors and the intent—sending ourselves on a new sensory journey.

Journal Exercise 7
ASSOCIATIONS

Most of our associations are being subtly led by either memories or by words or current situations. This exercise will help you see how much you are influenced by words associated with an image.

Try and work through each step below without skipping ahead. You may want to cover the prompts that follow as you work through step-by-step.

You will need: Your journal, a writing utensil, and a deck of tarot cards

Part 1: Revisiting the Table.
1. Go back and observe the table image (Image 4).
2. Write down the first image or words that pop up when you see that picture.
3. Now look at the table image and imagine it has the tagline "Complete."
4. Write down your observation of the table with this caption.

5. Now look at table image and imagine it has the tagline "Alone."
6. Write down your observation of the table with this caption.
7. Compare your observations from steps 2, 4, and 6. Does your perception of the image alter with the tagline?

Part 2: More Associations

1. Look at the following image (Image 5).

Image 5: Adding Tags to Images

2. Write down your first impression of what it represents.
3. Look at the image again but imagine the caption "Attack."
4. Write down what the image makes you feel now.
5. Look at the image again but imagine the caption "Endangered."
6. Write down what the image makes you feel.
7. Look at the image again but imagine the caption "Hiding."
8. Write down what the image makes you feel.
9. Compare all of your reactions to the image. Did the captions alter them?

Part 3: Tarot Associations

1. Pull a few cards from your deck. Note down the cards in your journal.
2. Write down how the cards make you feel. Also make a note of your surroundings and your current mood.
3. One week later, pull the same cards out again.
4. Write down how they make you feel. Also make a note of your surroundings and your current mood.
5. Compare your notes from steps 2 and 4.
6. Are your notes the same or different? Was the context (surroundings, mood, etc.) the same or different?

Contemplate: Do the labels on the cards or suit names alter your view of the cards?

Musings

I hope this chapter gave you some insight into how we move from looking at images to creating meaningful connections in the brain. Next time you look at a tarot or oracle card, or maybe even look for signs in the universe, pause a moment to observe the object that you are noticing. Then dwell on what details jump out at you and what you recognize immediately and what details you ignore. Become mindfully aware of what meanings and images pop up in your head immediately. Do these change as you observe closer? Then check your own mental state and emotional state to understand what you associate the image with. What made you move from the image to its associated context? How does that make you feel? I do not suggest you do this at every instance, but checking your practice every once in a while can give you a clue about your own thinking processes and help you hone your interpretive skills.

Now that we have meaningful images in our head, we will talk next about how we use these cues to make those intuitive leaps of faith and how we can reflect on them to gain insight to help us understand where these intuitive guesses came from.

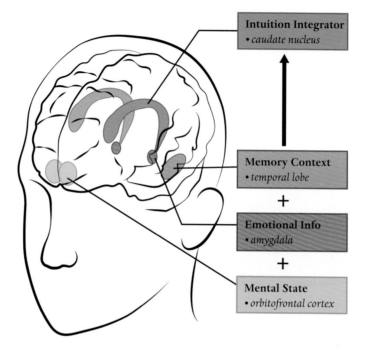

Illustration 4: Anatomy of Intuition and Insight

The intuition integrator (the caudate nucleus, green) puts together information incoming from the senses (yellow) that helps us recognize and categorize objects with our internal states from the orbitofrontal cortex (blue). Memory context (the temporal lobe, purple) is added to this integrator along with emotion processing from the amygdala (red). This is the complex processing in an expert intuitive. Novices just use memory (purple), from reading the book, for example, and their current mental states (blue).

CHAPTER 2
DELVING INTO INTUITION

Decisions, decisions, decisions. We rely on intuitive decision-making in our jobs, in our everyday lives, and most importantly, in emergency settings. Our lives are full of choices, and in many instances, we make these based on incomplete information but with the belief that the choice we make is the best course of action. In fact, if we have to wait to gather all the information, we will probably always be in a state of frozen stasis with no decision made at all. Many a diviner, be they a tarot card reader or astrologer, is approached by querents in this state of paralysis hoping to gain some clarity on potential outcomes and paths forward. It is a way to tap into their unconscious intuitive instincts.

A few years back, I was feeling stuck in a research lab. Things were going well, yet I felt stagnated. On a whim, I approached someone whom I had no connection with to see if I could collaborate with them. This person had no prior knowledge of me, and their work was in no way connected with what I did. But I emailed on the spur of the moment, and while I did not work with this person, they introduced me to a now good friend who transformed my life. Why did I make that first contact? What led me to approach this particular individual? Some intuition prompted me at that particular time in my life to make a specific move, which led to big changes.

Another way I have relied on intuitive connections over the years is through speed dating! I have met lifelong friends, a few boyfriends, and my partner through this activity. In many instances, the connection is formed in a matter of minutes, perhaps even seconds, with intuition leading the way. We are all like horses with blinders on, allowing gut instincts and hidden senses to guide us on forks in the road. The act of making decisions based on unconscious information is the concept of intuition. This is when the conscious brain is blindfolded and you make a choice. After the moment, you may be asked, "So, why did you pick option A?" and you may not know why, but something in you was saying that was the best path. Without these intuitive leaps, we would be stuck in an analytical labyrinth, waiting for the rational path out. Intuition is the thread (or in many cases a rope ladder or pogo stick) that can lead us out of this labyrinth.

Evolutionarily, this was needed for species to make split-second decisions to survive, and we still rely on this circuitry to navigate life. Intuition is learned over time, beginning in childhood. Even as kids, we have to start processing non-verbal cues like eye blinks, tone of voice, body postures, and gestures to intuit information about the mental states and dispositions of people around us. These lessons are then carried over into adulthood. We cannot always explain the reasons behind how we jumped to an inference. In some instances, these intuitive decisions are correct. We learn over time which decisions were right and which were not in order to develop our intuition and can say, "I just know!" While your intuition may not always be right, it tends to make you feel better that you made a choice.[7]

The site of intuition lies deep in the brain (Illustration 4). By now we have taken in all the sensory information from the outside, made our assumptions, and tied those with meanings and associations. But along the way, we have also observed some unconscious intangibles like body language, tone of voice, eye contact, our own biases, and maybe even the temperature in the room or the energy around us. Our brain takes in all of this, filters it into an intuitive guess, and resolves a problem. This resolution of the conflict makes you feel good and is termed positive effect. Maybe you will spend time later wondering what led you to guess a certain way or what made you go down one path and not the other; all that happens to gain insight much later. At this moment in time, intuition based on fragmented information is what is guiding you.

One easy example I can give for making an intuitive decision is when I decided to give up on buying an apartment. On paper it was a superb apartment—a three-bedroom unit in a great neighborhood with a very decent price. But when I walked in, there was this feeling that led me to decide that it wasn't for me. My partner and I actually bid on the apartment, got it accepted, and then walked away from it—all for that intuitive feeling. Looking back, the apartment price has gone up—but I have never regretted walking away. I do distinctly remember that I had a

_____

7. Zander-Schellenberg et al., "It Was Intuitive," 1505–13.

sinking feeling when I walked in, a draining of energies of sorts. How one would describe that I don't know. I also know that it was a time in my life when I was hyperaware of these signs as well.

Journal Exercise 8
EVERYDAY INTUITION

This exercises should help you zero in on how you use your intuition in everyday life.

You will need: Your journal and a writing utensil

1. In your everyday life, you take actions or make choices without knowing why. Write down a list of actions/choices that you recently made without knowing why.
2. Reflect on why you made such a choice.
3. In the next week, when you make a split-second decision without a known reason, write it down.
4. Reflect later on why you made that decision and write down plausible reasons for it.

Contemplate: How often do you make intuitive statements in your readings?

Journal Exercise 9
YOUR PHYSICAL EMBODIED INTUITION

Much of our intuition relies on physical responses, which usually go unnoticed. This exercise will get you noticing physical responses during your intuitive choice making. It is more about recognizing your "random" choices. Are there cues that you use for these? Some of us may be very attuned to these, while others may not, but it is important for you to know.

You will need: Your journal, a writing utensil, and a deck of tarot cards

Part 1: Your Body as Your Dousing Rod
1. Shuffle the deck of cards and split it into three piles.
2. Choose a pile. Do you gravitate toward one more than the others?
3. Write down how your body reacts and how you feel when you move toward the chosen pile. (Feelings can be happiness, sadness, a tension in your shoulders, a tightening in your chest, etc.)
4. Repeat step 1.
5. Again, choose a pile. Do you choose the same pile as last time, or is it a different one?
6. Write down your reason for picking the same or a new pile. Is it just a random guess or body guidance?

Part 2: Ignoring Your Choice
1. Shuffle the deck of cards and split it into three piles.
2. Choose a pile. This time, ignore your first choice and choose a different pile.
3. Write down how you feel. (Feelings could be a lightening of the heart, sinking of your gut, breathing easily, etc.) Did you feel any resistance or a change in breath?

Contemplate: Do you listen to your body during a reading? How?

An Intuitive Reading

Let us try a reading. I have recently been contemplating a career shift (or at least a temporary shift). I pull out a few cards for clarification.

Image 6: An Intuitive Reading: Three of Cups, Three of Wands, Page of Cups, Five of Cups, the Empress, and King of Wands

The Three of Cups, the Three of Wands, and the Page of Cups emerge first. For more clarity, I pull three more cards: the Five of Cups, the Empress, and finally, the King of Wands. I lay them out like a pyramid, the bottom cards forming the base of the decision, leading to the pointed outcome at the top (Image 6).

Based on my previous experience with these cards, their associative meanings and images, I have a positive feeling about this career move. The Three of Cups and Three of Wands talk about emotional, creative energies but also of a potential move associated with the change. The Page of Cups also points toward a message or an opportunity from outside. I am also feeling a sense of dread when it comes to the Five of Cups, looking at the loss of what transpired before and perhaps the burning of bridges. But the Empress, with her bountiful riches, points to a fruitful opportunity, and it all cumulates in the creative energy of the King of Wands.

Perhaps one reason why some say to not do readings for yourself is the difficulty in moving past our internal inhibitions in order to gain clarity of thought from the intuitive process. But divining for yourself, over time, can provide a good calibration of your emotional states, help clarify how you react to situational contexts, and reveal how you interpret signs. Think of it as a fun mirror into your brain. This reading, or my interpretation of the cards, is pointing toward the positives of the career change with the potential for some retrospective mourning of a life left behind. This particular reading did not require me to get "unknown" insights, as the images seem pretty clear, but that may also be an inherent bias of my own as I'm trying to psych myself into applying for an opportunity.

But *your* intuitive ideas for this same set of cards and my query could be different. Perhaps for a novice, looking into the books for individual meanings, the interpretation of the Page of Cups or the Three of Wands would have been more pedantic. Try it out.

Journal Exercise 10
YOUR INTERPRETATION

This exercise will help you dissect a reading based on your intuitive abilities. The hope is for you to begin to see patterns in your own leaps of faith and what they respond to. The more aware of these you become, the better you will become at understanding the intuitive leaps in your readings.

You will need: Your journal and a writing utensil

Part 1: Your Interpretation

1. Look at the cards in Image 6. Think of my question: What do you think about the possibility of a career change?
2. Write down how you interpret the cards.
3. Does the timing of this question matter, or will your interpretation be the same no matter when the query is asked?
4. Are the images of the cards enough, or is the context also important?

Contemplate: Do you do readings/divinations for yourself or close family members? Reflect on the advantages and disadvantages of reading for yourself. Think of your biases and blinders but also the fact that you may know yourself the best.

The Information Sieve

So, what knowledge are we applying when using our intuition? Our senses are feeding us a lot of information constantly. Although our brain processes it all, we don't have to be "conscious" of every piece of information received. In fact, it might be detrimental and result in overstimulation if we become cognizant of every minute detail that is processed by our brain. The unconscious mind puts together incomplete situational cues and internal emotional conditions, forms connections, and leads us to intuitive responses. Think of your intuitive brain as a sieve. When you are mining the world for knowledge, you collect ore with diamonds and gold but also a lot of sand and dirt. The brain takes in all of this, then shakes it in the intuition sieve to filter out all the junk that may not be needed in the moment. Finally, you are left with a collection of ore that you use to create narratives, patterns, meanings, and decisions. It is not to say that the chaff and the dirt that was thrown out is unimportant, but it is not needed right now to make the choice in front of you. You can also imagine that this brain sieve has larger or smaller holes depending on the situation and how much nuanced information you need to solve the puzzle at hand. But also imagine not having a sieve, loading up a pan full of clay or sand, and trying to sift through to find the right pieces of the puzzle needed to make a decision. You might be left meandering and searching through the mud for all eternity without a sieve! This is the power of the intuitive brain.

Imagine a line drawn from one temple on the side of your head to the other, going through the brain. Along this line and behind your eyes is the seat of intuition, the caudate nucleus (Illustration 4, green). We already spoke about how incoming sensory information gets tagged with meanings and memories in different parts of the brain. These tagged sensory details are passed along to the front of the brain where your internal gut feelings are also mapped (Illustration 4, blue). These are then integrated in the caudate nucleus to make intuitive decisions.[8]

Journal Exercise 11
INTUITION AND YOUR ENVIRONMENT

How much is your intuition influenced by environmental inputs? This exercise will help you attune to your internal states and recognize what influences or occludes your interpretations. Becoming aware of that threshold where your emotions override all other factors is important,

---

8. Cheng and Tanaka, "Developing Intuition," 17492–501.

especially if you don't want your own feelings to influence the query in front of you.

You will need: Your journal, a writing utensil, and a deck of tarot cards

Part 1: Interpreting the Environment

Try to go through step-by-step without looking ahead. If needed, close or otherwise hide the follow-up questions and next steps as you work through each one.

1. Close your eyes and take a few deep breaths.
2. Visualize a sense of calmness and peacefulness. At this moment, think of a question or problem that you would like a solution for. Open your eyes and write down the question.
3. Pull out a card from your deck, but keep it closed.
4. Look at the following image (Image 7) for one minute.

Image 7: External Influence I

5. Open the card that you pulled in step 3.

6. Write down your interpretation to the question you asked.

7. Now put away your card.

8. Close your eyes and think of the same question.

9. Open your eyes and pull out another card from your deck. Again, keep it closed.

10. Look at the following image (Image 8) for one minute.

Image 8: External Influence II

11. Now open the card you pulled in step 9.

12. Write down your interpretation of the card for the same question.

Part 2: Reflection

Based on these steps above, work through the following prompts.

1. Compare your interpretations of the cards.

2. Reflect on if your interpretations were influenced by the external images.

3. Try the same exercise by looking at the second image (Image 8) first, then repeat the steps using the same tarot cards. Are your interpretations different?
4. What comes first when you interpret? Your internal emotional state or the meanings and metaphors of the card.
5. Reflect on your answer above.
6. At what point do you say you are not ready to give a reading, realizing you are too influenced by external factors?
7. Try this exercise at different times of the day or days of the month. Take notes and see if patterns emerge. People have different hormonal cycles and biorhythms. You may be very sensitive to your internal cycles, which could affect your intuitive interpretations.

Contemplate: Where do you do readings? How does space influence your thoughts?

Body Rhythms and Intuition

As animals, we have different rhythms that shape our lives. We have the regular day-night cycle because of the sun, the monthly lunar cycle because of the moon, and seasonal cycles as the earth revolves in its orbit. Other creatures use these seasonal and diurnal variations to time various behaviors, such as nesting, mating, foraging, and hibernating. For the most part, our lifestyles have occluded our awareness of these different cycles that we experience as human animals.

We have biorhythms that change with the time of the day and are attuned to the day-night cycle that we experience. When I was younger, I grew up in a time without smart phones or streaming services. This is not to date myself but to give context to the level of external influences that could obscure my awareness of body/mind rhythms. I used to wake up at 4:00 a.m. all chipper and clearheaded to complete my homework and solve math problems. I also used to love teaching the 8 a.m. lab courses, with many of my students groaning about how happy I sounded that early in the morning. With changing life paces, doomscrolling, social media, and other distractions, my 4:00 a.m. wake-up call has become a thing of the past. But even now, when I want to accomplish certain tasks or focus, I love to wake up at the cusp of dawn to get things done. While some of you may relate to this, for others it might be the complete opposite. Maybe you get your best work done at midnight.

These differences in being active, aware, and focused depend on how awake your body is and how responsive it is to the world. This is termed as arousal state. Place a palm against the back of your neck where the skull meets the vertebra. Below there is the locus coeruleus, which releases the chemical norepinephrine that helps to control your daily biorhythms (Illustration 1, orange ellipse). There seems to be some evidence in increased creative/intuitive thinking in the evenings in some individuals and more analytical processing in the mornings in others. In many individuals, mind wandering, or freely moving thought, rises from the morning through midday and then lowers before rising back up in the evening. This wandering correlates with changes in norepinephrine levels in the body.[9]

Track your daily cycles with an hourly calendar to see when you get the most insight and are most intuitive. Is that something that can be correlated with external factors? How about people you regularly meet?

Journal Exercise 12
TRACKING THE BEST TIME FOR YOU

This exercise will help you gauge when you are at the best of your intuitive abilities. If you are a morning person, you may want to think about your mind wandering moments in the afternoon as a place for gaining insight. If you are a night person, the midnight hours may be the best for mind wandering.

Part 1: Assessing Your Productivity
Think about your daily routine and when you are the most and least productive. Think about your childhood and when you were the most

---

9. Smith et al., "Mind-Wandering Rates Fluctuate."

and least productive growing up. Also ask your colleagues, friends, or family as to when during the day they think you are at your creative best, physical best, and conversational best (and worst). Based on these inputs, reflect on the following questions, adapted from Horne and Ostberg.[10]

1. If you had no constraints, what time would you get up?
2. At what time would you go to bed if it was entirely up to you?
3. When during the day would you like to exercise?
4. When during the day do you feel your physical best?
5. When do you feel tired because of a need to sleep?
6. If you were to take a test, when during the day would you prefer to schedule it?
7. If you were to host a brainstorming session, when would you like that to be?
8. If you were to engage in a creative endeavor, when would you do it?
9. At what time of the day are you at your "peak"?
10. Are you a morning person or an evening person?
11. If you were to sit and journal, what time of the day would you choose?
12. If you were to tackle a vision board, what time of the day would you choose?

Part 2: Reflection

Reflect on the answers to the questions above and complete the following statements with regards to time of day/night. You could also answer with no preference. These are for you, and there is no right or wrong answer.

1. I am at my physical best usually in the _____.
2. I am at my creative best usually in the _____.
3. I am intuitively dialed in usually around _____.

---

10. Horne and Ostberg, "A Self-Assessment Questionnaire," 97–110.

4. I love to contemplate and ruminate around _____.
5. My analytical mind wakes up around _____.
6. My best divination sessions to read someone are usually in

   _____.

7. My daily life and my creative biorhythms are in sync. (Yes/No)
8. I would like to be more in tune with my rhythms by

   _____. (Think of some action items, say waking up
   early, scheduling calls in the night, etc.)

Hormonal Rhythms

Aside from biorhythms that all of us share, cis women may also have menstrual cycles. Do the changing hormonal levels during the menstrual cycle have effects on cognition and intuition? The main source of these hormonal changes are the ovaries, which release estrogen and progesterone in different quantities throughout the month (Image 9). Some studies suggest that cis women's abilities to recognize fear peak with their estrogen levels each month. It is also suggested that with increased estrogen there is increased dopamine in the striatum, which can help with sequential tasks.

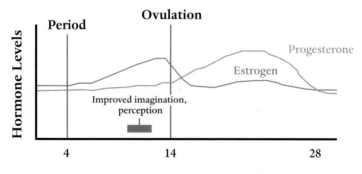

Image 9: The Menstrual Cycle

In cis women, there is a time window during the menstrual cycle when they seem to have increased levels of imagination, perception, and even fear perception. This is thought to depend on the rise and ebb of different hormones during the days of the menstrual cycle—estrogen (Image 9, blue line) and progesterone

(Image 9, pink line)—with estrogen being high during the high perception window (Image 9, green bar).

There does seem to be substantial evidence that just prior to ovulation cis women seem to remember minute details of even mundane events (e.g., how much was paid for a latte to the exact penny or dime or a specific arrival time at a spot down to the minute).[11] This is also a space of time where imagination, perception, and social abilities seem to be heightened. The time of the cycle just after ovulation is reported to be calmer (with increased progesterone) than before (with lower progesterone and higher estrogen). If you menstruate, it may be interesting to keep note of your cycles and try to see when you are the most perceptive or even receptive to external cues or nonverbal signals.[12] Keep a record of what details you notice at different points in the month and see if a pattern emerges. Are you then prone to more intuitive choices at certain times of the month? And then, looking back, are these choices considered the right ones?

The caveat here is that trans men and women and cis women who are past menopause are ignored in a lot of scientific studies, especially those related to cognitive abilities (though many of them are included in studies of "disabilities" such as dementia and Alzheimer's). Intuitive abilities of cis men are also not investigated given the social bias toward "women's intuition." Science has also been quite slow in moving beyond the gender binary and being truly inclusive in research practices. These are blind spots of the scientific community, probably due to the fact that for many centuries the realm of science research has been under the purview of cis men. We need to change this cycle, recognize the wisdom in our elderly, and have more studies pertaining to cognitive abilities of our older populations and be inclusive of all genders.

Mind Wandering

Many of us talk about going down mental rabbit holes. We dive deep into our realms of fantasy, worlds constructed entirely on metaphors that we have created over time. If you are an astrologer, perhaps you see the planet Jupiter as a gentle giant or can see the war clouds surrounding Mars. If you are a tarot

---

11. Maki, Rich, and Rosenbaum, "Implicit Memory Varies across the Menstrual Cycle," 518–29.
12. Gorvett, "How the Menstrual Cycle Changes."

enthusiast, you may have stories about the children in the Six of Cups and it takes you into a nostalgic memory. In your business, you may have noticed certain patterns that point toward particular trends or a set of events that makes you think of specific scenes. These cases of mind wandering are not just within the purview of divination readings. In fact, most of us are subject to mind wandering—it is a way for our brains to process the immense information that we are constantly bombarded with. We see things, create patterns and stories, and allow our mind to wander to make sense of what it all means.

Mind wandering seems to especially help when you have problems that don't seem to have an immediate solution or an answer. Instead of directly probing the problem, if you allow the mind to wander while doing a different mundane task, say washing dishes or cleaning your gutters, you may suddenly solve the puzzle in your head. Divination tools, such as tarot cards or charts, may be a different way of approaching the solution—or wandering to an answer.[13] Imagine a situation where you are stuck making a decision. If you dwell on the problem over and over again, that may result in worry, anxiety, and may even lead you down into depression. If you use a divination tool, say tarot cards, and use the imagery of the cards to guide your thoughts, this would be an instance of directed mind wandering, where we are imposing constraints on the flow of ideas. This kind of directed mind wandering has been shown to have benefits in creative engagement, finding meaning, and setting future goals.[14] This directed conscious wandering of thoughts is distinct from unconstrained dreaming.

While some amount of undirected mind wandering is good for the intuitive process, it can also be a way of zoning out or removing focused attention from the task at hand. It has been suggested that mindfulness meditation, as an exercise, is good for training the brain to avoid wandering and to stay the course. So, if you find yourself walking down tangents during a reading or divination exercise, you may want to practice some form of mindfulness. A simple method could be targeted focus on some aspect of the images in front of you to corral yourself back to the constraints of the reading instead of embarking on trivial pursuits. In fact, mind wandering, or doing nothing and allowing thoughts to bubble up, may help after a reading or divination practice to gain insight on

---

13. Christoff et al., "Mind-Wandering as a Scientific Concept," 957–59.
14. Smallwood and Schooler, "The Science of Mind-Wandering," 487–518.

what transpired before. While intuition may have led you to an answer, you don't know why you came to that reasoning, and mind wandering may help with understanding how you arrived at the end.[15]

The part of the brain that is responsible for mind wandering is thought to be the default mode network (Illustration 5).[16] Think of wandering your hands from your third eye to the top of your forehead. Start here and imagine diving in, splitting the brain in half. This is where the medial prefrontal cortex is (Illustration 5, purple). Move toward the crown and dive in deeper to find the posterior cingulate (orange). From the crown of your head, you can move diagonally toward the top of your ears. As you are about to fall off your skull, notice the lateral parietal areas (yellow). When we think about the future, our self, or of other people, these parts of the brain are engaged—which pretty much covers many divination sessions!

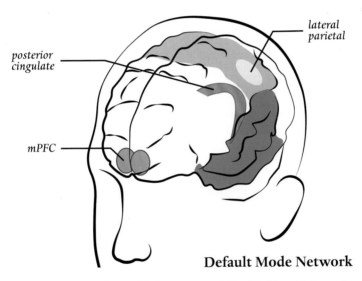

Default Mode Network

Illustration 5: The Self, Future, and Meditation Network

The default mode network (DMN) integrates information from multiple areas of the brain, a few of which are indicated here: the medial prefrontal cortex (mPFC), the posterior cingulate cortex, and lateral parietal areas.

---

15. Zanesco et al., "Experience Sampling of the Degree."
16. Wan et al., "Posterior Cingulate Cortex."

Divination, at its core, has people asking questions about themselves, about others, or about the future. Many of us look to divination to find a purpose or meaning for events that have transpired. Some look to cards and charts to glean ideas about future outcomes or the effects of choices. We also use imagery as a way to break free of cycles and find new perspectives that can help us resolve issues. Mind wandering has been shown to support all of these benefits.

Future Goal Orientation

Exploring future-focused self-generated thoughts that examine the barriers to goals and how they can be overcome is a good use of mind wandering or divination. Let us say you want to buy a car and are unsure of how and when you will get one. Thinking about it constantly is giving you hives. For this hypothetical situation, I pulled out two cards: the Seven of Pentacles and Queen of Swords (Image 10). I could interpret them as putting in the effort to reap the rewards and not feeling upset about not having achieved the goal yet. The Queen also speaks to focused action to reach a goal. So, perhaps instead of wasting time and effort wondering if the goal will be achieved, use that energy to be laser focused on moving toward your dream. This would be one way to use tarot/divination to direct mind wandering toward tangible solutions.

Image 10: Planning the Future:
Seven of Pentacles and Queen of Swords

Creativity

New creative thoughts emerge from mind wandering, and it is similar to that of a creative experience. It allows people to leap into divergent thoughts, find unusual uses for objects, and find transcendent solutions to problems. In some ways, it is a way for us to subvert reality and find new paths forward. I have recently felt stagnant in my job as a professor and have been struggling to reignite the passion for some classes. I asked the cards for a way to jump-start some ideas. I pulled out the Four of Cups (Image 11). Instead of immediately jumping into the interpretation, I looked at the image more closely, concentrating on bits I don't normally notice. At first glance, the Four of Cups has a cup held out from the clouds, being handed to a person contemplating three cups on the ground. As I looked at it longer, I got excited. My usual approach to teaching neuroscience is to start bottom-up and not cover topics such as dreaming or mindfulness, as the field is vast. This card suggests that one way for me to reinvigorate my classroom is to bring in more of these abstract, ephemeral concepts and not just the reductionist ones. It is actually an exciting approach that I think the students will enjoy.

Image 11: Jump-Starting Creativity: Four of Cups

Meaning

Mind wandering also allows one to add purpose and meaning to their experiences and place them in a new context. This results in better well-being. It is a way for us to create a narrative for life and find the story behind our choices and actions. As a neuroscientist, I have often wondered, "Why am I writing this book?

What is the purpose behind me delving into tarot and, even more so, researching and writing about it?" I pulled out a card to help me resolve this struggle within and got the King of Wands (Image 12). This, to me, says to be open about all of me and not hide my true self and desires—that to truly achieve my best, I need to embrace and celebrate all of me. And divination is a big part of that. It is actually quite a beautiful interpretation, and it makes me quite emotional. As I edit this manuscript, I realize that the King appeared before in a career reading (Image 6). And the suit of wands also seems to be a theme associated with this book and me. My mind is now racing to find connections and correspondences!

Image 12: Finding Purpose: King of Wands

Mental Break

If you find yourself stuck and not able to make such leaps of narratives, it might be time to take a break and let your mind wander and think about something unrelated. Card images can be really beneficial in letting you jump into random stories unrelated to the problem at hand, allowing you to take a mental break.

Mastering Your Intuition

We use our intuitive abilities all the time. For some of us, it is the basis of our professions. Doctors, athletes, and gamers become better at their skills and quicker in their responses by honing their intuitive abilities. Looking at brain images of young novice doctors and those with greater experience shows that the latter have much more complex brain activation and integration when coming to their decisions.[17] If you are untrained, you may be relying on a step-by-step manual of moving through the details, saying $1+1 = 2$, as opposed to jumping straight to the answer, perhaps also taking in more information.

Imagine an expert tennis player facing an opponent who is playing an amazing game. If the expert were to rely on calculated logic—"If I hit here, then the ball will land there, and the person across may do X, Y, or Z"—that kind of conscious processing will take too much time, before which the game will be finished. In fact, you can "see" novice players make those calculations and lose the game because they become stuck or overthink it. A veteran player, on the other hand, relies on past memories, anticipation of where the ball will land, and what the opponent will do. This is why they watch videos of opponents' games to take in different tactics, body cues, and other unknown factors that they can then use during the actual game. This allows them to act intuitively as opposed to consciously. This is what separates veteran athletes, who have heightened senses of anticipation about where the ball will go, from those just starting off in the field.

Doctors, anesthesiologists, and other medical professionals report similar actions—when they make a decision in the split of a second based on a hunch. Maybe it is the color of the blood or a certain smell or just the feel of the tissue as they cut in—but these factors are quickly processed by their subconscious brains to allow them to make quick life-saving decisions entirely based on their intuition. It is only later that they reflect back on it, while writing their reports, and identify what factors led them down a certain decision tree. And those reflective moments are now added into their intuitive pathways for the future.

Conscious decision-making takes over eight seconds, while unconscious, intuitive decisions can happen within a second. The caudate nucleus, which was mentioned as the main intuitive integrator (Illustration 4), is especially involved. It has almost no involvement at the beginning of training but heavy activation at the end of a training regimen. This is perhaps one reason why astrologers recommend apprenticeships. While many novice tarot readers may depend on the little books that come with decks, the more expert ones do not use them as extensively. Think of any activity that involves decision-making, such as driving a car, playing a new board game, parenting. Initially you may rely on books, advice, or peer input, but as you become more of an expert, it becomes more intuitive. You

---

17. Hruska et al., "Hemispheric Activation Differences," 921–33.

learn from the patterns, how situations unfold, and about the dynamics of others. In effect, if you want to become more intuitive—practice, practice, practice.

As a novice diviner, you are probably using associations and meanings from prior memory, perhaps relying on the information from a booklet and what you have been taught prior about the meanings of a particular image or chart (these memories/associations are in the temporal lobe). You are also relying a lot on your current mental state (the orbitofrontal cortex), which is coloring how you interpret the meanings that are being beamed up by the temporal lobe. As an expert, however, your processing is much more complex. You involve the emotion center (the amygdala), more object recognition and pattern recognition (parietal and temporal lobes), the internal calibrator (the orbitofrontal cortex), and the master integrator (the caudate nucleus) (Illustration 4). This last part seems to be the key to making those new complex intuitive judgments that cannot just come from a book.[18]

Journal Exercise 13
EXAMINING YOUR EXPERTISE

The following prompts will help you assess your expertise and contrast it with being a novice using new modes of intuiting. The hope is to give you an understanding of how quickly you process ideas using one modality versus the other (and how much one may depend on your reflexive intuition and the other on building up knowledge and book information).

You will need: Your divination tool of choice (tarot, oracle, etc.), a divination tool or resource you are not familiar with, your journal, and a writing utensil

1. Do you consider yourself an expert diviner or a novice?
2. Is there a specific tool that you use for your divination? If you do not use divination tools, write down in your journal what aspect

---

18. Wan et al., "Developing Intuition," 17492–501.

of your life you use intuition the most in (playing video games, driving, while working, etc.).

3. Try to learn a new tool for divining. Learn some simple aspects of palmistry or chart reading if you are a tarot reader; look up some oracle cards or clairaudition if you normally look at astrological charts.

4. Now think of a question.

5. Try to find an answer or clarification for your question using your novice divination tool.

6. Observe how long you take to come up with interpretations. Write down how often you refer to books or other resources when interpreting.

7. Now go back to your preferred (expert) tool system to answer the same question.

8. Observe how long you take to come up with interpretations. Write down how often you refer to books or other resources when interpreting.

9. Between the two systems (novice and expert), which interpretation do you trust more?

Contemplate: Are your quick, immediate divination responses better (or more accurate) than more considered ones?

How We Know What We Know

Intuition is one thing. It is a reflexive, spontaneous decision that makes you move forward. But this does not come with self-awareness or even logic. Making sense of what you did or how you chose comes much later—when you reflect upon your path and ask yourself, "Why did I choose that?" or "Why did that happen?" or "Why did I really just do that?" Many of my insights come when I take my morning shower. This is when I sometimes have a dialog with myself, articulating events, trying to make my unconscious brain talk to the conscious side, and suddenly the insight emerges: "OH! So that's why that happened!" Some folks call insight the "Aha!" moment generator. It's the point when someone whacks you on your head (albeit internally) and says, "That's why!" Unlike intuition, where there is not much information, in the case of insight, you start matching up the outcomes of your decisions with what may have led you there. The blindfold is finally removed from the brain and the light illuminates the decisions. This will then be added to your intuitive repository for the next time (whether you chose right or not).

This kind of reflective processing is important, as this is how we learn so that the next time we are faced with similar cues/signs we know how to respond. This is also a time for recalibration. While the intuitive guess may have provided you with a sense of contentment at the instance of decision-making, that choice may not have been the "correct" one. The reflective, insightful bit allows you to reassess, and do better the next time.

Intuition + Incubation = Insight

Let us take an example of a reading. I ask the question, "Will I finish this book on time?!!" I have been having a lot of stuck moments and misgivings about how to proceed. I quickly shuffle the cards and draw out the Nine of Cups (Image 13). It has the image of a man sitting below nine cups, smiling. If you have looked up meanings for this card before, you would have seen things like "getting what you want" and "accomplishing your goals." At first blush, it is a great reading, and for the moment, it leaves me with a sense of hope that all will be well. It could also be a way for me to self soothe, and whatever the card may have been, I could have interpreted it to give myself a sense of appeasement to allay my anxieties for the moment.

Image 13: Seeking Clarity: Nine of Cups

As just an exercise, I tried to interpret a random image (Image 14) to assess the same question.

Image 14: Further Clarification: Rose on Swing

In this case, I have no past associations with the image or any booklet to convey its meaning. This is how I interpret the image: while the world looks bleak, there is a bright bloom to be picked up as an offering. Again, it seems very positive regarding the outcome of the project. Even though my mind seems stuck (and there is no movement of the swing), there is the prospect of a beautiful outcome.

So, what am I looking at in the image? Here are my notes: I see the black and white and its contrast to the pink flower. I know that I feel bereft of ideas, and that is what I associate the black and white with. I also note that the swing is stationary and not "moving," again indicating how stuck I feel with the writing process. But the main object is the pink rose. It is interesting to me because normally I associate roses with funerals, as Indian funerals usually have roses as garlands, and I am not a huge fan of roses or their smell. But that was not my first thought. Instead, the rose's colors, contrasted against the black and white, stood out to me like a beacon of hope and not as the cloying sweetness I normally associate with the flower. Also, the pink color was like a first blush—it was unlike the red roses that I normally loathe. Even though the image displays symbology that I would usually not like, I appreciate the symbols in this context and interpretation.

All this is going on in my head—with no words, with no prior connotations—and yet it is so evocative! We use our visual cues, memory centers, and associations to come up with some meanings, and our intuitive brain then makes leaps, perhaps with aid from booklets or other sources or just your expertise on what the situation is about. This then eases the "tension" in you with regards to the problem at hand. This intuitive positive effect makes you feel good at the moment. All this happens pretty quickly and mostly at an unconscious level. At this point, if I asked you why you said one thing or chose another, you would probably say something like, "Because it is just right," "It made me feel good," or "It was the right choice."

Then you dwell on it and perhaps ruminate as to why a particular choice was made, and then it percolates over time. As you think about it more deeply, you may either gain some logical insight as to how you arrived at a conclusion or simply experience revolutionary insight, where it just hits you without working through the logical steps. The mind wandering we described before is a good way to gain revolutionary insight. The best part is that now this insight is being added to the intuition integrator (the caudate nucleus), allowing you to use it the next time! I will have to revisit these images of the Nine of Cups and the rose after I finish the draft of this book to see how I reinterpret them, and if my intuition was right.

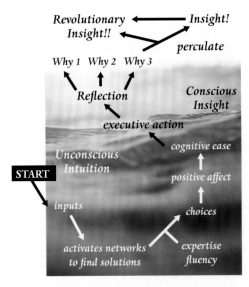

Image 15: Moving from Intuition to Insight

A lot of intuitive processing happens unconsciously. But it involves your expertise and fluency in the subject matter. The intuitive decision gives you a sense of ease—a resolution of the quandary at hand. From there, the conscious insight processing takes over. We ruminate on the whys and why nots and finally gain insight into the situation (Image 15). Sometimes these insights jump steps and you get mind-blowing revelations (think big scientific discoveries or creative ideas).

The brain regions involved in the reflective systems (insight) and the reflexive impulsive systems (intuition) are different. The memory centers (hippocampus), object recognition (temporal lobe) and location centers (parietal lobe), and the decision-making centers (prefrontal cortex) are heavily involved in the reflective pathways, which makes sense as we are recollecting events and trying to make sense of what happened in a step-by-step manner. The reflexive systems are tied to emotional centers (the amygdala), the intuition integrator (the caudate nucleus and nucleus accumbens), and parts of the frontal cortex (Illustration 6).

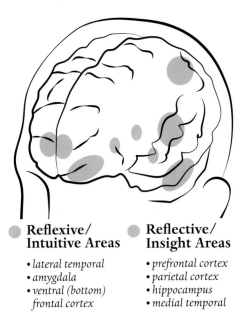

Reflexive/ Intuitive Areas	Reflective/ Insight Areas
• *lateral temporal*	• *prefrontal cortex*
• *amygdala*	• *parietal cortex*
• *ventral (bottom) frontal cortex*	• *hippocampus*
	• *medial temporal*

Illustration 6: Reflexive and Reflective Pathways

The areas that are involved in unconscious intuitive processing, which is reflexive, (pink) are distinct from the insight generation pathways that are more reflective (blue).

Journal Exercise 14
USING YOUR INSIGHT

Insight is reflecting upon our intuitive choices. The following exercise, adapted from Handler, Campbell, and Martin, will give you some tools for stepping through your insight to gain intuitive clarity.[19] Constant revisiting can give you a better understanding of influences on your intuitive decisions.

You will need: Your journal, a writing utensil, and a friend or two

1. In your journal, draw a house, a tree, and a person (take two to three minutes).
2. Now, examine your sketches. Think about why you drew them this way. Is this how you always draw these things?
3. Write out your observations.
4. Ask a friend to go through steps 1 through 3.
5. Share your sketches and compare how they look.
6. Compare notes on why you each drew your pictures a certain way.
7. For the next month, at the beginning of each week, draw a house, a person, and a tree—each time without thinking too much about it. Then reflect on the drawings and what they invoke.

Contemplate: Does reflecting on your intuitive, instinctual responses help or hurt your process?

---

19. Handler, Campbell, and Martin, "Use of Graphic Techniques," 387–404.

DIVING FURTHER INTO YOUR INTUITION AND INSIGHT

This exercise will train both your intuition and your insight. You may want to alter this exercise using everyday objects that you have and try to understand what they convey to you. It is a form of active listening.

You will need: Your journal, a writing utensil, and a deck of tarot cards

1. Pick a tarot card and look at the image for five seconds. Close the card.
2. In your journal, doodle the first thing that came to mind when you saw the card. Or write down the first word that came to mind. (This is the intuitive bit.)
3. Now think about why. What in the image prompted you to respond this way? Was there something you noticed in the card that triggered this word or image? (This is probing for insight.)
4. Return to the card from step 1, open it, and contemplate on it for five minutes. Close the card.
5. Again, write or doodle whatever came to mind.
6. Observe what you wrote or drew. Is it different from what you wrote or drew before. Why or why not?

Contemplate: How often do you change your thoughts upon reflection (during or after a reading)? Does insight alter your intuition?

Seeking Insight

Sometimes we may get stuck in readings. Even if the spread is in front of us, we may have some niggling lack of clarity, some missing piece. Sometimes the message comes later—when we are not actively searching for it. This insight is the result not of analytical, conscious reasoning but of a subconscious problem-solving that has percolated to the top. Where do we go looking for such insight? For Archimedes, the bathtub worked, and it literally hit Newton on the head under an apple tree. I usually am hammered by insight in the shower, and it looks like there is a whole slew of investigative studies as to why people gain insightful ideas in the bath. Many seem to also get these while washing dishes or doing mundane tasks that allow your brain to switch off its "conscious mode." The trick seems to be to allow your mind to wander but not too much. In Buddhist traditions, insight realization through intuition (as opposed to reasoned realization) is termed *abhisamaya*. These insights are far-reaching and termed as prelogical, but they arrive at truths. It is also said that lessons learned from these realizations are not as easily forgotten as those learned through a step-by-step approach to understanding.

Stuck in a Loop?

There are instances, however, when insight is forever elusive. Dwelling on the question directly—"Why did I do that?" or "Why did I say this?"—may only make the answer slip away further. So, how can we wrangle the monkey brain of ours to share its secrets? Here are some prompts for you to use to tackle your brain and wrangle insight, adapted from Sawhney and Khosla.[20]

Finding Differences: Ponder a difficult question/decision/behavior that you made or something that confuses you. Think back to a choice you recently made but did not know why you made that particular decision. Were you or others surprised by the choice that you made? Were there things different about your reaction to this situation compared to prior times/contexts? What was different this time? Find the anomalies.

Life Intersections: What about other things or events that were happening at the time of your decision? What other actions or choices did you make that

---

20. Sawhney and Khosla, "Where to Look for Insight."

were unrelated to this specific question? This can be a pattern emerging from the intersection of narratives in your life. At certain points in my life, I have found that every activity I do needs to be redone or revisited. Otherwise, things come with ease or with a certain struggle. We all go through such phases, and it would be good to recognize those patterns.

Stubborn Beliefs: What were your expectations of the problem or situation at hand? Are you being stubborn in your thinking? Do you always hope for the same exact outcome? Are you failing to recognize how things have changed? Asking these questions will help you challenge your own beliefs and ingrained behaviors.

Inserting Randomness: Try to ignore exploring the problem and the choices you made to solve it. Think of something completely random or different and let your subconscious mind ruminate on what you did. Or go to a new location and let your mind dwell on the question at hand in a different environment. The changed context can help you chance upon the insight. The part of the brain that can come up with these leaps of insight (beyond logical reasoning) could be tied in with creative thinking.

Journal Exercise 16
GETTING UNSTUCK

Sometimes we get stuck in a reading and fail to understand what it means. These exercises can help you jolt out of usual ruts.

This exercise has many parts. It may help to do just one part, take a break, try the next part later, and so on.

You will need: Your journal, a writing utensil, and a deck of tarot cards

Part 1: Anomalies
1. Pick a tarot card that you are familiar with.
2. Look for something unusual in the card. Is your eye drawn to a specific location that it hasn't been before? Was there a different feel to pulling the card out of the deck?

3. Contemplate on these answers.
4. Write your observations down in your journal.

Part 2: Intersections of Narratives
1. Shuffle the deck and pull out a few cards.
2. In your journal, write down observations about themes and relations between the cards.

Part 3: Orthodox Beliefs
1. Pick a familiar tarot card.
2. In your journal, write down your immediate interpretation of the card. Is your interpretation of this card the same each time?
3. Think of a scenario when this card would mean something different. Write it down.

Part 4: Changed Context
1. Think of a question.
2. Shuffle your cards and pick a card.
3. Write down your interpretation of the card and how it answers your question.
4. Move to a different location or think of a different question.
5. Look at the same card again.
6. Does the altered context change the way you interpret the card? Write down your observations.

Part 5: Analogies
1. Think of a question.
2. Instead of using tarot cards, pick out three objects from your immediate surroundings.
3. Write down your observations of these objects and how they relate to one another.
4. Use these analogies to interpret your question.

Contemplate: What is your go-to strategy when you encounter a complex reading or choice?

Musings

All of us are intuitive—that is the only way we can interact with the world around us. Otherwise, we would be stuck in one place, paralyzed by decision-making. How do we recognize the ways in which we process intuition? How do we become better at using our intuition? Sometimes we may be led astray by our intuition. Our brain serves as an information sieve that takes in a huge load of information and then makes split-second decisions. Using logic and calculated assessment of situations may not always be fast or clear enough in the moment to make those choices. The caudate nucleus serves as an integrator of different brain inputs, including your current mental state, which allows you to make intuitive decisions. In that instance of decision-making, intuition allows you to move forward so you don't have to worry your brain about that problem anymore (cognitive ease). It may not have been the right choice in terms of outcomes, but it was necessary to move forward.

In divination using tarot, astrology, or other symbols, we make such intuitive choices. While intuitive decisions and choices are important, it is equally crucial for us to learn from these and reflect on our judgments. This is how we become better at our intuitive processes and stop relying on just book knowledge, becoming true experts in our intuitive abilities. Insight can be transformative, and it can be a logical reasoning of how we went about choosing A over B, or it can just leap out at us from out of the blue.

I hope this chapter gave you some tools for attuning to your intuition, allowing you to become more aware of what you notice, and steps to become more insightful. Next, we will talk about layering emotions on top of what you perceive and how your emotions flavor your metaphors and intuitive decisions.

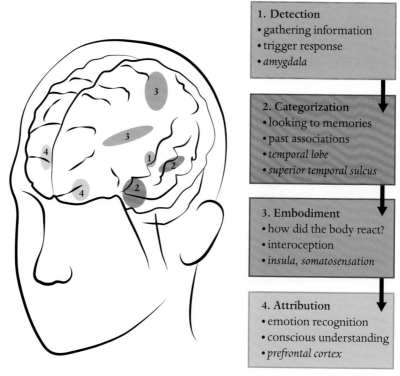

1. Detection
- gathering information
- trigger response
- *amygdala*

2. Categorization
- looking to memories
- past associations
- *temporal lobe*
- *superior temporal sulcus*

3. Embodiment
- how did the body react?
- interoception
- *insula, somatosensation*

4. Attribution
- emotion recognition
- conscious understanding
- *prefrontal cortex*

Illustration 7: Anatomy of Emotions and Interoception

Emotion processing is complex and involves both the brain and the body. At the center is the amygdala, which is the main emotion detector. Our body reacts to situations, and its responses are coded in the insula and calibrated against previous emotions we have experienced. Finally, we attach tags using the cortex and can then express our feelings.[21]

21. Spunt and Adolphs, "The Neuroscience of Understanding," 44–48.

CHAPTER 3
EMOTIONS AND INTEROCEPTION

Why do we have to talk about emotions when we talk about divination? Aren't the intuitive flashes we use to form narratives just the subconscious tapping into some divine energy? On the contrary, I find that the emotional state of the individual heavily influences the interpretation of the signs and symbols. We are a whole being, not just a brain but a brain-body entity (some may even refer to the connection as a heart-brain or gut-brain connection) that responds to the signals we perceive from the external environment. Further, a lot of times when a person asks a question about a choice or a particular event, the outcome is emotionally charged. Why am I not happy? What is causing this anger? Will I feel fulfilled? Each of these questions has some tinge of emotion associated with them.

Body Metaphors

How many times have you looked at an image or a symbol and noticed a sinking feeling, felt a heaviness in your shoulders or something that makes your stomach clench, or let out a breath of relief. When talking to others, how often do you describe your emotional state with bodily metaphors? When you look at others, do you notice their body forms or postures and make judgments about their emotional states? A lot of our emotional processing happens in relation to our physical beings.

Journal Exercise 17
EMOTIONAL BODY AWARENESS

The following questions will make you aware of how much your body is involved in your feelings. Research has shown that intentional noticing of body changes can train you to become more aware of your inner physiological responses. Try to answer the following questions.

You will need: Your journal, a writing utensil, and a deck of tarot cards

Part 1: Body Language

1. In your journal, describe a few ways in which you use your body parts to describe emotions (e.g., my heart feels heavy, my stomach turns over).
2. Look at what you wrote in step 1. Do you actually experience these changes to these body parts? Or are these expressions just figures of speech you use?
3. How aware are you of these bodily changes for specific feelings?
4. Have you made decisions based on these bodily responses?

Part 2: The Body Tarot

1. Shuffle your deck and pick a card. Look at it for a minute or two.
2. Notice how you react to it in your body. Write about what body parts are relaxed, tensed, hot, cool, etc. Comment on your breath, heartbeat, and stomach.
3. Observe whether you felt a certain emotion when you picked the card.
4. Repeat this exercise for a few cards.

Contemplate: Where are your hands and feet during a reading? Do you place your hands against different body parts when making choices?

Encoding Emotions

I drew the Moon (Image 16) randomly from my deck. As we discussed earlier, tarot cards are just 2D images that we perceive and attach ideas and stories to, creating emotional valences with them. Maybe you have done numerous readings where the Moon card has portended something amazing. Perhaps many of your life events have been associated with specific details of the moon cycle. These are some of the flavors that accent the image you create.

Image 16: Emoting with the Body: The Moon

When I look at this card at this moment, for some reason I feel very breathless. I am holding my breath, and all the activity feels like it is happening in my head—something that I interpret as "cerebral." It makes me feel like I want certain things or have some hope, but the physical manifestation of it is constrained. As I continue to look at the card, I take a deep breath and release it—and notice the knots unwinding in my body. While my initial focus was on the moon and the creatures looking up to it, now my focus shifts to the water and the lobster creature slipping out of it. There is still some clenching in different parts of my body, but the big constraints seem to have dropped.

I have to note here that it is unusual for me to devote this much time to noticing individual body parts when doing a reading. But the intentionality behind these observations opens up a whole slew of questions and answers. When I interpreted this card as "feeling hopeful" and "looking inside," did I consciously process the fact that I had almost shut off my body and was in my head, so to speak? Could I interpret the card as "taking a pause, a breath, to help understand the situation at hand," which would mirror how I reacted, initially feeling breathless, then taking those deep breaths to release the knots? The body, in this case, serves as the blueprint for what I feel. Also, as an aside, how appropriate that the Moon appears when introducing a section about emotion!

Say you see something that you really love. You feel a flush in your face, your heart beats faster, your pupils dilate, and you may smack your lips. So, what makes you have these whole-body responses? Your holistic response to situations, when multiple areas in the body simultaneously respond, is because of the hypothalamus and pituitary. If you stick a pencil up your nose (not advised!), you will hit the pituitary and then the hypothalamus. Pulling the brain out through the nose is how Egyptians removed it during mummification processes, as they thought that the brain was not important in either this life or the afterlife.

These structures trigger cascades that are autonomic, or not under conscious control, so they occur immediately and in a very coordinated fashion, allowing for an orchestrated response across organs. Also, this ensures that similar stimuli trigger similar responses—it cannot be that anxiety at one time will cause you to hyperventilate and at a different time cause you to breathe freely. This way, there is no disconnect between the emotion and the body response.

Sensation to Emotion

When we say "it makes me angry" or "it makes me sad" or "I am happy," what do we mean? Let us look at a scenario. Imagine you walk into a room and you are asked to take a lie detector test. How will you feel? You hear the words, and you can see the test machine on a table with a lamp hanging over it. You take in the information, and your sensory systems convey it to the cortex, which makes sense of the words and the setting you have walked into (Illustration 8, step 1). From there, the cortex passes the information to the emotion processor (amygdala), which tags certain information to the scenario (step 2). Perhaps most movies you have watched with this setting didn't end well, or maybe the term *lie detection* has a certain memory or fear association within you. From here, the information is passed to the hormonal gateway for whole-body responses, the hypothalamus (step 3).

So, how do you react to this situation? You may start hyperventilating and show heightened pressure in your head. These would be symptomatic of increased breathing and blood pressure. The hypothalamus triggers such responses. The hormone norepinephrine is elevated to create a whole-body tenseness. Further, your eyes may widen, taking in more information around you, which is caused by a dilation of the pupils, an autonomic nervous system response. You may also express through your body. Maybe there is a frown on your face or the slump of your shoulders (step 4).[22]

Finally, the limbic system sends all this information back to the cortex to parse out what it all means (step 5). It is clearly a negative emotion—perhaps one of frustration and anxiety. The brain then has to decide what to do. You may decide to leave the room, as you want to avoid facing this negative emotion. That is the behavioral outcome. While this kind of holistic response may not always be triggered in a reading, even minor changes in our system are interpreted as one emotion or another. We are constantly calibrating and recalibrating our environment to assess how we feel.

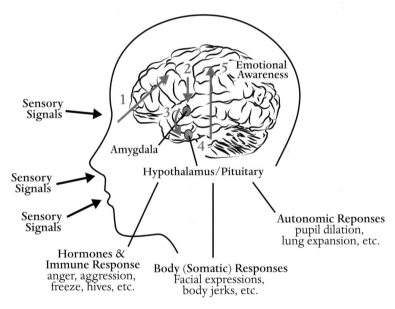

Illustration 8: The Pathway from Sensation to Emotion

Step 1: Information coming in from the sensory systems first goes to the cortex and gets processed.

---

22. Seth and Friston, "Active Interoceptive Inference."

Step 2: Then it is sent to the emotion processor (amygdala) and other centers that compare it with previous associations and offer a context (hippocampus/temporal lobe).

Step 3: It is then sent to the hypothalamus.

Step 4: The hypothalamus evokes a whole-body response by activating the autonomous nervous system (think heart rate, pupil dilation, lung expansion, etc.) and a somatic and immune response, as well as a hormonal, or endocrine, response (such as releasing stress hormones).

Step 5: The information from the emotion processor (amygdala) gets sent back to the cortex for "awareness" of the emotion.

Interoception

Let us go back to the Moon card (Image 16). Aside from the eye taking in the image, I also mentioned that I felt breathless and "cerebral." Think about how you felt when you saw the card. Any internal sensations were not a figment of your imagination. There are actual sensors in your lungs, heart, and other organs that determine how much they expand or contract. When you feel breathless, in most instances there is an actual contraction of the little nodules in your breathing tubes that are constricting the air.

While we rely on our perceptual senses (sight, smell, taste, touch, hearing) to get information from the external world, we also rely on our internal senses, or interoception, to understand what is going on within the body. Both of these "senses" are important when responding to different environments and situations. Interoception refers to sensing bodily changes and is tied to emotional processing and cognition. Interoceptive awareness arises from inputs or sensory information that comes from within the body. This is distinct from proprioceptive signals, which give you positional information, and the common senses of touch, smell, taste, hearing, and sight. Mechanical, chemical, and pressure information is sent from internal structures, which also get inputs from the nerves and blood.[23]

When you say that you have butterflies in your stomach or that you feel lighthearted, these interoceptive signals, or information from your internal organs, get sent back to the brain via the vagal nerve. The signals are then processed in the

---

23. Barrett and Simmons, "Interoceptive Predictions in the Brain."

amygdala as well as the cingulate cortex. The main hub of your internal representation of the body in the brain lies deep within it and is thought to be really important for human consciousness; it is called the insula. Even here, while signals are processed, they do not yet have "names." Your brain is able to integrate different body signals and put them together—but they have not been "encoded" or labeled. That finally happens when one becomes aware of a specific emotion, which happens in the orbitofrontal cortex. This is where you can say "I feel happy," "I feel joy," or some such. Aside from this, we also respond with stress and hormonal activation (via the hypothalamus) and with emotion processing (via the amygdala).

Let us say that you are scared of dogs and the sound of a dog barking makes you anxious. You walk into a room and hear a bark. This lets your brain know that there is a possibility of a dog. Given past experiences, your brain sends information to increase your heart rate and prepare you to freeze or run. Your response may be different if you saw the dog behind a cage. Also, your brain compares how you react to how it predicted you will react and categorizes the threat based on current information. Even if there is no dog, it takes a while for the body to settle back down to a neutral state. The insula gets information from what the current state of the body is (heart rate, lung capacity, etc.), as well as what the brain predicted it would be based on incoming information. It compares the two and decides—okay, this was either more or less stressful than what was anticipated.

Interoception in a Reading

So, how does this affect a reading or the divination process? Sometimes when we have a baseline level of energy going, it may render us anxious or excited or sad. This then sets the tone for your reading. You have a certain baseline heart rate, and then the reading alters it. Perhaps you also associate certain images and cues with certain situations; that may cause some coloring of the interpretation. Awareness of your body state and energy levels at the beginning of the reading, and then their alteration upon seeing the cards laid out, becomes part of your emotional response during a reading. Understanding these changes in your body and how you respond to them can help you become more intuitive.

People seem to have different sensitivities to their interoceptive sensations.[24] What if I asked you, "How fast is your heart beating right now?" What would you say? Not everyone can clearly say how fast their heart is beating. But if you

---

24. Garfinkel et al., "Knowing Your Own Heart."

start intentionally noticing it and training yourself, you can get pretty accurate at knowing how fast your heart is beating. We use such information to also notice how much air our lungs have (breathlessness) or monitor pain perception. This is to say that we can get better at noticing these internal aspects of ourselves and realize that this is how we "perceive" emotions.

Journal Exercise 18
BECOMING INTEROCEPTIVELY AWARE

Answering the following questions will help you learn about how attuned you are to your internal senses. Hopefully this exercise will make you aware of how much you know your own body and thereby recognize different emotions that arise.[25]

You will need: Your journal and a writing utensil

Part 1: Assess
Answer these questions to the best of your knowledge. It is okay to say you're unsure or that you don't feel anything.

1. Do you recognize when you are tense?
2. Where in your body do you feel the tension the most?
3. When you walk into an uncomfortable situation, how does your body respond?
4. In an uncomfortable situation, what parts of your body freeze up or relax?
5. Imagine you are in the comfort of your home or some relaxed environment. How does your body respond?
6. Do you distract yourself from discomfort?
7. Are you always aware of your breathing?

---

25. Mehling et al., "The Multidimensional Assessment of Interoceptive Awareness."

8. Do you know when your breathing becomes faster or slower?
9. Aside from physical labor, when have you found your breathing to be affected?
10. Do you normally perceive pain?
11. Do you power through pain or withdraw immediately?
12. How does your body react when you feel pain?
13. When you are in a conversation with someone, do you notice how you stand?
14. Can you easily focus attention on your body even while doing other tasks?
15. How does your body react when you are angry?
16. How does your body react when you think something is wrong?
17. Where do you feel it in your body when you experience joy?
18. How does your body react when you are calm?
19. Do you trust your body?

Part 2: Reflection

After answering the previous questions, reflect on and complete the following statements.

1. I am most aware of my body when I feel _____ (anger, joy, etc.).
2. My body awareness is mostly related to _____ (my breathing, my heartbeat, my muscles, etc.).
3. The emotion I need to become more aware of my body experiencing is _____ (anger, pain, joy, discomfort, sadness, etc.).
4. During divination, I tend to feel _____ (anger, pain, joy, discomfort, sadness, etc.).

Areas Affected in Emotion Processing

If I looked at just your brain activity right now, I would not be able to say what you are feeling. Let us think of our emotions during a reading. We lay out a spread and look at the images. These images, and the metaphors they convey, trigger bodily responses. These send information about touch, body position, movement, and chemical changes that affect the core of the body (Illustration 9, orange). Even though we feel something in the body, it does not mean that we understand what it means. This process of understanding (conceptualization) happens in the prefrontal cortex (red). This is where the narrative of what we feel is formed and we can think, "Oh, I feel this way because this is what I see." Even so, at this point, it is an abstract concept. To articulate this and express how we feel, we use verbal centers and executive action centers (purple). Finally, we also visualize what we feel. If I verbalize that I feel sad, I also have a mental image of what that means (blue).[26]

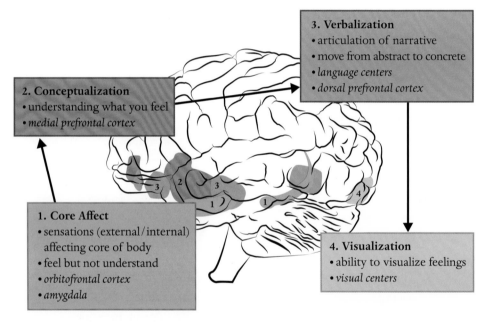

3. Verbalization
• articulation of narrative
• move from abstract to concrete
• *language centers*
• *dorsal prefrontal cortex*

2. Conceptualization
• understanding what you feel
• *medial prefrontal cortex*

1. Core Affect
• sensations (external/internal) affecting core of body
• feel but not understand
• *orbitofrontal cortex*
• *amygdala*

4. Visualization
• ability to visualize feelings
• *visual centers*

Illustration 9: Step-by-Step Guide to Recognizing Emotion

26. Barrett et al., "The Experience of Emotion," 373–403; Lindquist et al., "The Brain Basis of Emotion," 121–43; Kober et al., "Functional Grouping and Cortical-Subcortical Inter-actions," 998–1031.

Working through these questions will give you a sense of whether you react first with your body or your mind and at what level you attach labels to your emotions. This will help you recognize minute changes when you are doing a reading.

You will need: Your journal, a writing utensil, and a deck of tarot cards

Image 17: Exploring the Emotions of Cards: Nine of Swords

1. Observe the Nine of Swords and write down how you feel.
2. As you look at the image, think about what bubbles up first. Document any words/labels describing the image or bodily reactions to it (a feeling of tension, sinking of the heart, etc.).
3. Lay out a few cards from your deck.
4. For each of the cards, observe your heartbeat and your breathing.
5. Write whether your senses for light, sound, smell, and touch increase or decrease.
6. Write about your gut. Is it clenched or loose? How about your arms, legs, and other body parts?

Contemplate: What "body part" do you rely on the most for intuition? Gut, breath, heart, etc.

Wheel of Emotional Responses

We feel a range of emotions in a variety of brain regions. Sadness is felt deep in the brain in the insula, fear is felt in the amygdala, and happiness is experienced in parts of the frontal cortex.[27] Activation or deactivation of brain circuits does not equate to the pleasant or unpleasant quality of an emotion. In fact, some positive emotions, such as peacefulness and calmness, are caused by reduced brain activity or deactivation. Similarly, when you feel angry or tense, it is because of over activation of some brain areas. Some emotions activate brain areas, while others tend to deactivate them (Image 18). Absence of neural activity is not a bad sign.

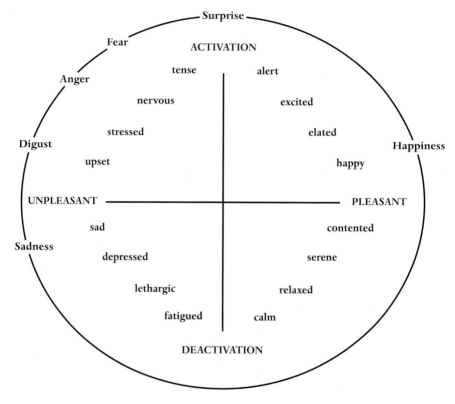

Image 18: Wheel of Emotions

---

27. Kragel and LaBar, "Decoding the Nature of Emotion in the Brain," 444–55.

One thing we may notice is that individual cards and the symbols themselves have no specific emotions associated with them. Our attribution of values such as happiness or sadness to such images is entirely dependent on our own internal states. Others may feel the opposite, believing that the imagery of each specific card/symbol (or its associations) evokes the same exact feeling each time. Both of these (and the spectrum in between) are valid ideas. It would help us, as diviners, to be aware of this range of emotional interpretations. Similarly, if you consider different planets to be malefic or benefic, you may have conjured up different images in your head and associated them with specific emotional qualities. But these are just ideas—you can create them and uncreate them as well. Next time, make a note of the context in which a symbol that you normally associate with one emotion evokes a different one. One example for me is the rose, which we spoke about briefly in chapter 2. Normally, I associate it with funerals and sadness. The sweet smell of roses is cloying and evokes deep sadness. But the same symbol, with its color changed to pink or as the only image in a black-and-white photograph, evokes a sense of hopefulness.

Journal Exercise 20
SYMBOLS AND THE EMOTION WHEEL

Use this exercise to find whether you associate certain symbols in your tools to certain emotions.

You will need: Your journal, a writing utensil, and a deck of tarot cards or other interpretive tools

1. Using Image 18, lay out your tarot cards (at least the major arcana) or other interpretive tools (say representations of the planets or zodiac signs). Place them along the wheel based on how they make you feel. If you are unsure how a certain card/object/symbol makes you feel, set it aside and continue.
2. Once you are done placing your tools, take a picture or make a note in your journal.

3. Revisit this exercise when you are in a different mood. Write down if your mood affects the position of the tools on the emotion wheel.

Contemplate: Consider using this wheel as a way to ask the querent how they feel about an outcome, or ask them where they would place the cards.

So, Where Is Emotional Attribution Done?

Emotions are first detected in the limbic system, with the amygdala getting information from different centers (Illustration 7, step 1). From there, we need to recognize what we feel, so we look to our memories, experiences from before, and past associations to categorize what we feel as emotion A, emotion B, or emotion C and so on. This happens in the memory centers in the temporal lobe (step 2). Then we look to see how the body has reacted to the current situation at hand. Is it what we expected? Did we anticipate fear but instead are just showing reactions for disgust? The insula has the information of the body reactions (step 3). Finally, these are sent back to the prefrontal cortex to say, "I feel this way because of this" (step 4).[28]

Where in Your Body Do You Feel Emotions?

Studies have shown that many people feel emotions as activations and deactivations in specific regions of their body.[29] Feelings of depression may leave you feeling cold in some areas of your body. Perhaps you don't feel your legs or your hands. Maybe when you are brimming with happiness, you literally feel your heart full and the chest area activated. Perhaps when you are excited, you notice tingling in the tips of your fingers or electricity running through your body. Or when you are deep in meditation, you might feel disembodied. In the following journal exercise, try to see where in your body you feel activation or deactivation. Use color crayons—blues and greens for cold/deactivation and reds and

---

28. Spunt and Adolphs, "The Neuroscience of Understanding," 44–48; Salzman and Fusi, "Emotion, Cognition, and Mental State Representation," 173–202.
29. Nummenmaa et al., "Bodily Maps of Emotions," 646–51.

yellows for warmth/activation—to understand where in your body you feel the most "activity" when you think of sadness, happiness, etc.

Colors the Area that Are

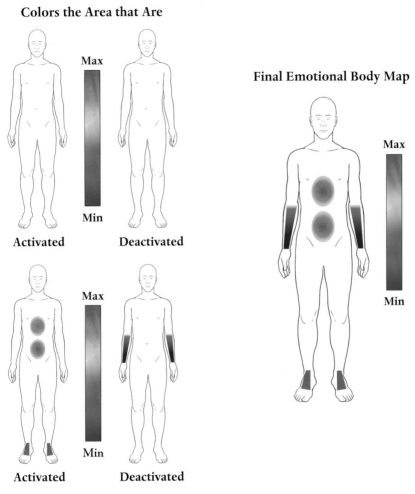

Image 19: Emotional Activation of Body Maps

Interestingly, studies have found that similar patterns of activation and deactivation occur in humans even across cultures. Where do you feel activated (stronger, reds/yellows) or deactivated (weaker, blues/greens)? For example, here I quickly mapped out where I felt activation or deactivation for feeling "happy." I closed my eyes and thought about what parts of my body increased or decreased in activity (Image 19).

MAPPING YOUR EMOTIONAL BODY

Use this exercise to understand where in your body you feel emotions. How do you (your brain) interpret activations and deactivations in your body? Next time you do a reading, try to notice if these body signals accompany your thoughts.

You will need: Your journal, a writing utensil, coloring crayons, a deck of tarot cards, and a friend or two

Color the Areas that Are

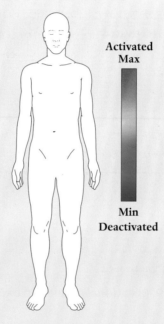

Activated
Max

Min
Deactivated

Image 20: Template Body Map

1. Use the body map as a template to indicate where you feel activated or deactivated for different emotions (anger, sadness, happiness, etc.).

2. Ask friends and/or family to fill out body maps for the same emotions and compare your maps. See if you all have similar activations/deactivations.
3. Pick five random tarot cards.
4. Color your activation/deactivation patterns when you look at each of these cards (one map per card). If you are an astrologer, you may want to color your activation/deactivation patterns when contemplating your chart or each planet/zodiac sign.

Reacting to the Body

Sometimes we are affected by emotional incidents or cues long after the initial event itself. Many times, we feel these aftereffects in our bodies. This is another reason to understand how your body reacts to emotions or, rather, how your brain processes bodily signals for different emotions. Imagine yourself walking into a darkened room. You notice something creeping along the corner across from you. While you notice this with your peripheral vision, when you turn toward it, you cannot see what the object was. This already triggers different aspects of your perception—the visual system and also the bodily autonomic and hormonal reactions that are preparing for a response to the situation. Perhaps you have had bad experiences with spiders or with darkened rooms in the past. Based on the information gathered, the brain is plotting through different scenarios and predictions of what may happen next and is trying to see which ones are most possible.

At the same time, your body response takes over—increased heart rate and breathing, maybe sweating and other aspects. While the body response is quick, the fact that these changes are happening is slowly sent to the brain stem, the thalamus, and the insula. Here you compare notes—what you expected to happen with your body given the current situation and how your body actually responded based on the situation at hand ("Oh, it's just a spider," or "It was just a small cat—calm down"). But this process is slow. Even though your brain is asking you to calm down, it may take the body a while. Thus, an emotional remnant lingers after the initial response.

In a reading, this could have different ramifications. If you walk into a room stressed or expecting some kind of anxiety, that may then cause your body to tense up, setting a baseline tone for a particular reading. Despite how strongly the cards or symbols may point in other directions, what the head says and what the body feels may have a disconnect. This also is important to recognize in the person you are reading for. If they anticipate or are looking for a certain outcome, that is going to color how they process the way the cards appear, your interpretation, and what that means to them. It will be important for you to set the tone of the reading. Before performing the reading, perhaps take a few deep breaths to clear the air. Do a quick body check to see where the knots are, and generally be aware of what your internal states are before you dive in. Think also of clearing exercises to complete after you finish your reading. Just like method actors find it difficult to shake off characters, someone who is very interoceptive could feel their body continue to perceive certain emotions after the divination exercise.

It may also be interesting to ask your querent to draw a body emotion map and indicate where they feel activated and deactivated, both before and after the reading. This will give them a sense of awareness. You will also notice if there are significant changes that their body kept score of during the course of the reading. Was there relief of stress? How about a settling sadness? Even if the querent may verbally say what they plan to do or what they heard from the reading, their body may be responding differently. This could help both you and them clarify what was heard and what was unheard during the course of the divination.

Journal Exercise 22
TYING EMOTIONS TO THE CARDS

This exercise will let you know where you feel different emotions in your body. It will also reveal how long it may take you to "recover" from certain emotional states or how long the aftereffect lingers. There are no right or wrong answers. Just awareness.

You will need: Your journal, a writing utensil, and a deck of tarot cards

1. Pick a card.
2. Observe how you feel when you look it.

3. In your journal, write where you feel activated/hotter or deactivated/colder in your body (or color a body map template).
4. Step aside for a few minutes.
5. After a few minutes, write down how you feel. Are you still affected by the card you looked at before?
6. Wait until you return to an unaffected, neutral state, then observe the card again.
7. Is there ever a disconnect between how you feel in your body and what your brain is telling you?
8. Let us say you pull out the Ten of Cups. Imagine your brain is telling you it should make you feel happy, but the actual image makes you feel (in your body) wistful? In this case, which information would you trust more?
9. Take at least a five-to-ten-minute break. Repeat this exercise for two more cards.

Contemplate: Is there a theme to your body activation/deactivation when you contemplate different cards?

Emotional Perception and Manipulation

So, now we know that emotions play an important role in our interpretations and tie in with the intuition we develop. How can we alter them? Can we become more body aware and manipulate emotions so as to have the best possible reading outcome? Do grounding exercises and meditation prior to a reading actually have effects on how we interpret cards, or are they just exercises that have no basis in scientific fact?

It looks like there is ample evidence that simple body postural changes can have tremendous immediate impact on your emotional state and thus how you respond to a particular scenario. Think of power postures (where you sit with your legs stretched, hands behind your head) or defensive postures (where you cross your arms and legs). These tend to immediately alter testosterone and cortisol levels.[30] The defensive posture reduces testosterone and increases cortisol

---

30. Carney, Cuddy, and Yap. "Power Posing," 1363–68.

(stress), with the opposite effects for the power pose. So, it would behoove us to intentionally adopt an open pose in order to be calm and open-minded during the divination process. Even if you set yourself up, be aware of mirroring that may occur with the querent; we may copy their posture, thereby altering our own body rhythms and emotional mind.

In theater, this form of internal emotional manipulation is done frequently. Actors are asked to imagine themselves to be big or small, expanding or contracting themselves within by using their body as a vehicle to convey the emotions. What has been interesting to find is that these bodily postural changes actually have an internal effect on how you perceive yourself and the hormonal changes that course through you. We can test this with an affect grid (Image 21).

Journal Exercise 23
AFFECT GRID

The affect grid has unpleasant to pleasant feelings on the left to right axis, and high arousal (how awake/aware you are) to sleepiness on the vertical axis.[31] When you are super excited about something, that leaves you energized and rates high on both the arousal and pleasantness scale. If you are super stressed about something, you may still have agitation because of a nervous energy, but it ranks low on the pleasantness scale.

Use this grid, adapted from Olenina et al., to assess how much your body influences how you feel and how quickly you get affected by it.

You will need: Your journal, a writing utensil, and a deck of tarot cards

––––––––––
31. Olenina et al., "Embodied Cognition in Performance."

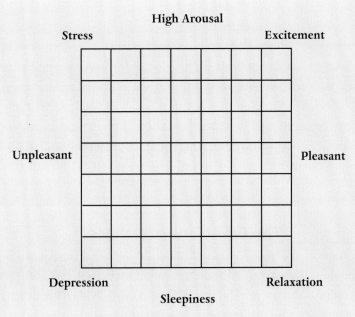

Image 21: Affect Grid

1. Place an X in the affect grid based on your current state. You can mark this book or draft a grid to use in your journal.
2. Walk around the room in a relaxed manner or sit in a relaxed posture. Assume neutral emotions. Where would you place X?
3. Imagine your energy radiating from the center of your body. Raise your arms, lengthen your torso, and imagine yourself expanding. Where would you place the X?
4. Imagine yourself contracting into a ball, withdrawing energy from outside. Shrink within yourself. Where would you place the X?
5. Pick three tarot cards. Observe the cards. For each of them, place an X on the grid. Reflect on where you placed the Xs and why.

Contemplate: You may want to think about using the affect grid exercise prior to a divination process to shrug off any bodily remnants of emotions before. It may also be useful for you to ask your clients (either in person or virtually) to also rid themselves of their current state and move to a more neutral or positive state prior to the reading.

Acknowledging your affective state during a reading becomes especially true when we become unreceptive to information. When we close in on ourselves, we do not want to "hear" what the other person has to say and assume a defensive posture that moves us toward anxiety. These body exercises can help us open both our bodies and our minds to new information, allowing us to change and adapt. If you have visualization tools that can help you with clearing the air or protecting yourself, be diligent about them.

The Emotions of Others

Till now, most of the book has talked mainly about the diviner and not really their response to a querent. But most divination happens in response to some-body's question—and not just the words but also the individual's body language, their tone of voice, and other minute details that we take in. Do the emotions of others affect us? If you see someone showing disgust, your brain networks (in the insula) will also respond with a disgust emotion. Even though you are not physically experiencing the situation, you can still "feel" it. Your brain seems to mirror activity based on what is perceived. Some of us are more susceptible to the emotions of others.

Journal Exercise 24
PERCEIVING EMOTIONS OF OTHERS[32]

Using this exercise, adapted from Doherty, may help you understand how susceptible you are to the emotions of others and whether you need to insulate from such influences prior to a divination.

You will need: Your journal and a writing utensil

---

32. Doherty, "The Emotional Contagion Scale," 131–54.

Part 1: Sadness

1. When you are talking to someone and they start crying, how do you respond? Do you get teary eyed? Are you stoic?
2. If you are experiencing a sad moment in a story or a movie, how do you react?
3. During a reading, do you respond to the sadness of your querent?

Part 2: Happiness

1. If you feel sad, does being around a happy person pick you up?
2. If someone smiles at you, do you smile back? How does it make you feel?

Part 3: Love

1. How do you feel when you are looked at lovingly? Touched lovingly?
2. How do you react when you encounter love expressed during a reading?

Part 4: Fear

1. How do you react when people around you are stressed or afraid?
2. If you look at fearful images in cards or elsewhere, how do they make you feel?

Part 5: Anger

1. How do you feel when you have a quarrel or disagreement?
2. When you encounter anger in a reading, how do you react?
3. If you encounter angry images, how do you feel? How does your body react?

Part 6: Reflection

Based on your answers above, complete the following sentences and reflect.

1. I am most affected by the emotion of _____ (sadness/happiness/love/fear/anger).
2. I tend to block out the emotion of _____ (sadness/happiness/love/fear/anger).
3. I feel _____ (sadness/happiness/love/fear/anger) more in my body than other emotions.
4. I need to become more aware of _____ (sadness/happiness/love/fear/anger).

Musings

When asked, "How are you feeling?" we may think that we are talking about how the brain feels—but there is more and more evidence that the brain is just interpreting and verbalizing the physiological responses of the body. Most divination answers involve emotional responses or require behavior that triggers emotional outcomes. In many ways, every reading is coded with emotions. We use metaphors to describe the symbols, and each of these carries emotional significance. We talk about love and hate, war and peace, balance and calm—none of this is emotionally uncharged. With this chapter, I hope you gained an understanding of how you encode emotions and where you feel different things in your body. It should have also helped you become more aware of the most powerful sensory system that you have—your own interoceptive awareness.

Many of us may also get all up in our heads during the divination process and not realize that our body is conveying something else, possibly through the clenching in the belly or a tightness in the chest. Even though our first instinct may be to interpret the card or symbol in a certain way, it could be that our body is pointing us in a different emotional direction. The hope is that these exercises will help you recognize those cues and allow you to pause and contemplate on them until it becomes an innate awareness over time.

Also, we need to remember that both the querent and the reader are human. They are living a reality where the reading is just a small event, and every reading is going to be affected by all the emotions and the energy we bring to it as a shared experience. While I am not asking you to become petrified stone, I do think embracing a sense of calmness or removing some agitation during the reading can help you process your own thoughts—especially if you are susceptible to emotional contagions. Your querent will also be more receptive to new thoughts and ideas if they approach the reading from a more neutral state. I hope you have gained some tools for that.

In the next chapter, we will delve into the transactional, social aspects that arise between a reader and a questioner during a divination.

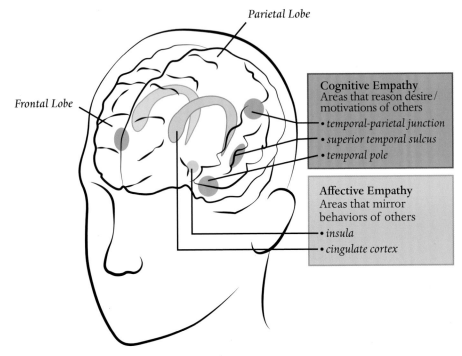

Parietal Lobe

Frontal Lobe

Cognitive Empathy
Areas that reason desire/
motivations of others
• *temporal-parietal junction*
• *superior temporal sulcus*
• *temporal pole*

Affective Empathy
Areas that mirror
behaviors of others
• *insula*
• *cingulate cortex*

Illustration 10: Anatomy of the Self and the Other (Social Cognition)[33]

We use two approaches to empathy—affective empathy and cognitive empathy. Affective empathy is used to feel what the other is feeling by mirroring their behaviors. Think of wrinkling your nose in disgust when you see someone else do that or crying with someone. Affective empathy is processed in the insula and cingulate cortex (which are both deep inside the brain). Cognitive empathy is used to reason out desires and motivations of others by putting yourself in their shoes. It is also termed mentalizing. Cognitive empathy is processed in the temporal lobe (along the side of your head, from your temples to the back).

33. Jankowiak-Siuda, Rymarczyk, and Grabowska, "How We Empathize with Others."

CHAPTER 4
THE SELF AND THE OTHER

Divination, or other forms of oracular insight, can be a self-reflection process used to understand oneself. However, many of us practice divination to answer queries from seekers. This is an interesting process, as we not only are creating mental images from the cards but are also processing information from the person in front of us—how they look, how they stand, how they speak. And now, working in a virtual world, perhaps we imagine how they look, picture their posture, and parse out the tone of their question from an email or voice. Some readers ask for a picture along with the query, and others may ask for additional objects. Some of us go in blind with just an astrological chart or a card spread. We have spoken at length in the previous chapters about how our minds use these tools (cards, charts, pictures) to create meaningful associations, tag them with our own emotional labels, and then make intuitive leaps to form substantive narratives and choices.

What we tend to ignore in most parts is that while the diviner says something, the querent is listening—and can take away whatever they wish from the reading. What they hear will be different from what is being said. Some of them may not be in the right frame of mind to either "listen to" or comprehend what is being interpreted in the reading. In that way, every reading for another person is transactional. This is limited by the vocabulary of the diviner but also by the comprehension of the querent. This is not to slight or diminish the capacity of either one but to ascribe the fact that their mental state and sensory systems also act as a filter, adding another layer of complexity to any reading. How can we resolve this? One way is to use tools like active listening, which allows the diviner to reflect back on what they said as well. In this case, you would ask the querent, "What did you hear from the reading?" or "What did you take away?" These are not leading questions like "Was that accurate?"

or "Does that resolve issues?" but more so descriptive questions that allow the querent to actively respond to how they heard your words.

At a workshop at the Omega Institute in 2023, I had the honor to present with Mary K. Greer, prominent tarot expert, prolific author, and the writer of the foreword to this book. One exercise she suggested we work on is trying to see what the querent sees in the cards, which is done by simply asking them to describe—not interpret—the cards in front of them. We went around the room working in pairs and realized that even among folks who have used tarot cards for years, just the shift in perspective revealed so much. So, ask the querent what they see. Many times the querent may notice nuggets that you, as a reader, may not have seen, and this may reflect their current state of mind.

Narrative Engagement

Can you make a story based on the following three images? Think about your narrative story and write it down in your journal. I contemplated on them for a little bit, and this is what I came up with:

> The land has a lot of history, with civilizations that lasted over centuries. Over time people lost a sense of their past, and art that was once pristine started to lose value and became derelict. Eventually even the rudiments of this were lost and were paved over to develop more practical spaces like fields of astroturf, creating new objects of worship and glorification, sports and commerce as the new religion. What people did not realize was that this was a slow, progressive burn of their essence being cut off, sliced up by themselves. Each cut caused a lot of pain but tolerance built over time, so even that pain became endemic, the sense of loss now a part of the DNA.

Image 22: Making Narratives from Images

Now, this is a story narrative I came up with in five minutes, building some kind of coherence around the three images. The images themselves are disparate, thematically unlinked and aesthetically very different, and yet my brain filled in the narrative gaps. Forming such narrative coherence from bits and pieces of information is something we do all the time. We make sense of behaviors around us and even our own memories by constantly constructing and rejecting narratives from a steady stream of information over time. As we encounter new information, we create a new movie/plot around it and then use that as a model to make sense of the world. Sometimes, this plot is accepted, and at other times, it is revised. For these events in the plot lines, we also need to form connections between cause and effect—events that unfold because of other influences.

The structure of any divination reading is a story. Perhaps we are telling the story to ourselves or to the querent. When we lay out a set of tarot cards in a spread or unfold an astrological chart, there is always a question or problem, some choices, and outcomes. And then the images and metaphors that we see will conjure up a narrative arc. So, how does our brain respond to such a narration? People respond better and are better engaged with a narrative arc when they can follow a beginning, middle, and end.[34]

In many ways, spreads such as the Celtic cross, or even a simple past-present-future spread, can build these arcs. The frontal-central lobe of the brain, especially in the left hemisphere, shows high degree of neural activity during

---

34. Dini, Simonetti, and Bruni. "Exploring the Neural Processes."

engagement with narratives. The other area of the brain that is actively engaging in narrative construction, mental mind travel, and scene construction is the default mode network, which we prior discussed as essential to mind wandering (Illustration 5).[35] As the querent engages these parts of the brain while listening to a reading, they are constructing the plot and adding to the narrative being unfolded by the diviner. We have to keep in mind that while the diviner is using the cards to narrate the story, the querent or listener is the one with the fuller picture. The situation at hand is their life, their emotions, and only they can fill out all the details. While some of these particulars may be veiled in the subconscious, the listener controls how the plot unfolds.

Journal Exercise 25
DIVINER–QUERENT TRANSACTION

At what point does the narrative change from when a diviner interprets and talks about an image to when the querent hears and processes what was said? Use this exercise to walk step-by-step through the speaker-listener transaction. It will help identify what bits of what you say are the most engaging and when your listener zones out!

Work with a friend. You can take turns serving as the querent or the diviner. Ask a question or state a problem, and then use your tools (cards, charts, etc.) to answer the question.

You will need: Your journal, a writing utensil, a deck of tarot cards, and a friend

1. Acting as the diviner, pull out three cards in response to a question/problem posed by the querent.
2. Write down what you observe as a diviner/reader.
3. Ask your querent to write down what they see from the cards.
4. Now narrate your reading of the images/cards. Ask your querent to repeat what you said in their own words.

35. Simony et al., "Dynamic Reconfiguration of the Default."

5. Note the differences and similarities between what you said and what they heard. What points of your narration stuck with them? What points were ignored?

6. Ask the querent to narrate how this card reading is seen in the context of their entire life situation (facts that you do not have access to).

7. Ask if your narrative arc was engaging. How much did they pay attention? Where did they gain the most interest and when did they lose interest?

Contemplate: Do you recognize when you have "lost" a querent during a reading, when they are no longer listening to you? How do you know? Sometimes querents nod along but do not agree with what you are saying. How are you aware of that?

At the Crossroads of Someone Else's Mind

When does someone seek a reading? Usually there is some kind of conflict or unresolved situation. If we think of the querent's life as a story, the point at which they approach a divination reading is a crossroads. From this junction, multitudes of futures could emerge, for which they need clarity. Imagine you are planning to meet a friend for dinner. In your head, you can picture how the evening will unfold. Perhaps you can see yourself leaving on time and arriving at the restaurant early. You can also picture the traffic on the way and see yourself getting stuck in it. In each case, you can also imagine how you will feel, including how your friend will feel if you arrive late. This looking ahead to the future is called prospective cognition, and it involves the default mode network.[36] All of us do this prospection all the time, using information from our current situation and memories plus other pieces of information to simulate future events so that we can plan the next steps and deal with them. So not only are we laying out the different aspects of the plot and future developments but we are also integrating that into what the storyline will be in the future. Wander your hands along the midline of your head, toward your

---

36. Konishi et al., "Shaped by the Past."

crown, and imagine slipping inside. This region (the precuneus) and also the memory regions along the side of your head just above your ears (the temporal gyri) are important for this plot integration.[37]

Many of us may also have encountered or can remember readings when we went in anticipating a certain answer and came away with a narrative that we just could not digest. Sometimes, even as the cards are being laid out, we create our own interpretations inside, and they might be completely different from what the diviner says. In many cases, we may remember such discordant narratives in great detail. This happens when we cannot reconcile the information we hear with what we expected. When we "resist" what we just heard in a reading or cannot find a way in which that model fits with our world view, it will be very difficult to change our minds in the moment. This is because we have created our own future versions in our heads and what was heard does not match up with those visions.

The default mode network is highly connected to the "self" (Illustration 5). When we hear narratives that are discordant with the self, this network is under activated and the system that is involved in judgment-related tasks is turned on (the fronto-parietal system).[38] This causes us to reject the plotline or narrative proposed. There is lack of comprehension of how the pieces of the puzzle fit at this moment, but it may be put together at a different time point. Take a step back to see if there is any logic or basis to what is being said.

Journal Exercise 26
DIFFERENT VERSIONS OF A READING

We may be unaware of how future-oriented the brains of querents are (and they may also be unaware of how they are conjuring up different versions of the future when you lay out the cards or the chart during the divination process). This exercise will help you understand how much the querent's own brain is affecting how your narratives are interpreted. You can perhaps also witness the fight between their

---

37. Song, "Cognitive and Neural State Dynamics," 8972–90.
38. Tylén et al., "Brains Striving for Coherence," 106–14.

default mode network and the fronto-parietal system if you provide discordant narratives to what they envision.

Work with a friend for part 1. You can take turns serving as the querent or the reader. Ask a question or state a problem and pick some cards to answer the question.

You will need: A friend, a deck of tarot cards, a writing utensil, and your journal

Part 1: Getting into the Querent's Story

1. Have the querent ask a question or state a problem, then have the diviner draw three cards.
2. After the diviner narrates the vision from the cards, ask the querent what it means for them immediately.
3. Ask them how the interpretation will then affect their future/next steps and how they envision the choices unfolding. This will give some ideas behind what the plot is and how it fits into the life narrative of the person in the future.
4. Does the diviner's version of how things will unfold match up with how the querent thinks things will unfold?

Part 2: The Discordant Reading

1. Do you remember a reading where you were in complete disbelief with what was said or when the reading was contradictory to everything you believed in?
2. Write down how you felt and how you reacted during the reading.
3. Has there been a time when you were the reader and the querent did not agree to your interpretations?
4. How did they respond? What was your reaction to their response? Did you get a chance to see how things unfolded?

Contemplate: What is more important for you in a reading—your version of the interpretation or what the querent is interpreting in their heads?

Empathy

One question we face during a reading is whether we are tuning into the emotions of the querent in front of us—and, in many cases, also if the querent is reacting to our own emotions. We now know from research that observing another person's pain can affect or trigger similar networks in our own brains, thereby mirroring the feelings experienced by others.[39] We spoke briefly about the emotional contagion that can affect us and how some of us are more attuned to this than others. Our brains have the capacity to distinguish "the self" from "the other" (mainly in the right superior marginal gyrus, or rSMG), and this separateness helps us to usually avoid the emotional contagion. This sense of separating the self from the other is greater in adolescence (with greater activity in this area of the rSMG) and decreases as we get older. This may be why we develop greater empathy as we age.[40] We also have the ability to understand the pain that is being felt by others or respond to the fear of others (think of why we enjoy or can relate to scary movies). The ability to mentalize the pain of others is thought to be present in the temporoparietal junction of the brain (the TPJ), the seat of self-awareness (insula), and the area affecting impulsive actions (anterior cingulate cortex, Illustration 10).[41]

Let us say you are getting ready for a reading. The querent comes in and looks agitated. You immediately picture some event that has caused this person to experience anxiety or frustration. When you imagine another person in a certain emotional state, you activate a "representation" of that emotion within yourself! Not only do you picture the emotion of the other but you may also respond to that with appropriate facial expressions or body movements. Think of someone opening a door to see a surprise party for them. How will they react? Can you picture the widening of eyes, lifting of eyebrows, and maybe jaw dropping? How does your facial expression alter to "surprise"? All of us do this as a way to understand and recognize the emotional responses and facial expressions of others. This is how we "feel" someone else's emotions. This is one step in the empathic process and is termed affective empathy (Illustration 10). But we also have the ability to go beyond just the face value of seeing someone showing emotions. Perhaps you see someone look scared when they are on

---

39. Gilbert, "Compassion as a Social Mentality," 31–68.
40. Riva et al., "Emotional Egocentricity Bias Across the Life-Span," 74.
41. Jankowiak-Siuda, Rymarczyk, and Grabowska, "How We Empathize with Others."

the top floor of a building. Your first response is to recognize the fear on their face and understand the emotion it conveys. But beyond that, you may think, "Oh, maybe this person fell from a height before" or "Maybe this person feels dizzy when they are up high." You start elaborating on the scenario causing the emotion. We have the ability to understand the desires, intentions, and motivations of the other person. This capacity to delve further into the emotion of the other is called cognitive empathy (Illustration 10). Imagining the life of the other is not easy, but yet we need to do this on an everyday basis—not just with close friends and family but with folks all around us. It involves feeling things that the other feels and also imagining what they may be going through.

To do this, we must have a picture in our head of what the other may be experiencing, what the motivations behind those emotions are, their sources, and what it would entice them to do. We are creating a mental scene of how the person sitting across from us will react to different scenarios. This is called mentalizing. During a reading, mentalizing is a two-way street. The diviner/reader tries to mentalize and create emotional pictures of the querent, trying to empathize with them and offer narratives based on these scenarios. As these different possibilities are being narrated, the querent forms their own plots for the future, mentalizing the emotional states of their own future selves, such as "This choice will make me happy" or "This choice will make me unhappy."

Social Cognition

Humans, being social creatures, have had an extensive history of trying to make sense of the behavior of others and predict how they are going to act. How we make sense of another's behavior, how we calibrate how people perceive themselves, and how it relates to our own self all form the crux of social cognition. In many ways, this is the core of what happens in a divination reading between a reader and a querent. The reader is trying to make sense of the actions, choices, and behaviors of the querent, while the querent themselves is filtering this information through the lens of how the reader speaks, how they formulate the narrative, and their demeanor, tone, and body language. Social cognition is like a detective exercise—we have to decode information like facial and emotional expressions but also make inferences on the mental states of the other in order to make intuitive decisions. These are detective tactics that we start learning from when we are toddlers and keep improving on through our entire lifespan.

As we do not have direct access to someone else's thoughts and thereby cannot predict their actions, we need to have some means of understanding what people intend to do. We need to be able to understand the mental state of people around us—what are their beliefs, desires, and life experiences? We then create a mental representation of the brain of others, and it is distinct from the mental representation of ourselves. We use these mental representations to analyze and predict the behaviors of others. This kind of mental representation (mentalizing) is not completely innate. While some of it can be seen in infants, much is learned over time, beginning around age four. This is a little different than empathy, when we tend to mirror or feel how someone else reacts to a situation or mimic their emotional expressions in our own brains, triggering autonomic or body responses.[42]

As you can imagine, the way in which we "decode" people in front of us is not simple. First comes the layer of perception of facial expressions, gestures, body postures, language, and voice. This social perception (Illustration 11, step 1) helps us take in and integrate the face and body cues from others. This is then integrated to understand their affective state (trying to empathize with the other person). We do this by trying to feel what they are feeling and evoke mirrored responses in ourselves (step 2). We also try to codify their behaviors/words/demeanor in terms of metal states (step 3). The areas that are involved in social perception in step 1 do not activate during actual action—but rather only when we are trying to understand the meaning behind the actions of others! These details, along with our emotion centers and our current mental states, help us code the emotional content of our observations. "Does *this* mean they are happy or sad or disgusted?"

The mirror system and the mentalizing system are distinct from each other and offer complementary information. While the former is about observing the action of the other or how they hold themselves, the latter is trying to infer information on how they will act or why they acted a certain way—how will they express a feeling as opposed to why they will express a feeling. In a reading, you are using your mirroring system to understand what the querent is feeling and responding to how their dynamic changes. You then use the mentalizing system to figure out the reasoning behind actions, motivations, etc.

---

42. Arioli, Crespi, and Canessa, "Social Cognition through the Lens."

Step 1
Social Perception

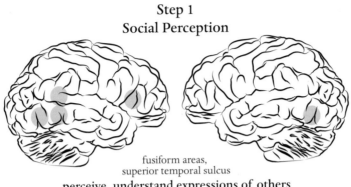

fusiform areas,
superior temporal sulcus

perceive, understand expressions of others

↓

Step 2
Mirroring

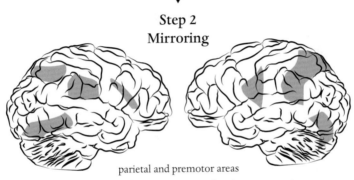

parietal and premotor areas

activate internal imagining and mirror emotions

↓

Step 3
Mentalizing

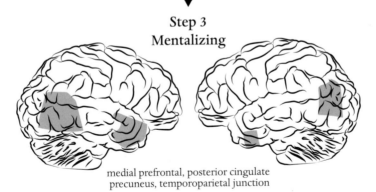

medial prefrontal, posterior cingulate
precuneus, temporoparietal junction

understand motivations and desires of others

Illustration 11: The Layers of Social Cognition

First, we need to recognize what is going on with the other person, identify facial features, and try to understand the meaning behind what the other person is doing (Illustration 11, blue). Then we try to empathize with the person by mirroring their emotions or actions (say frowning when the other person does or smiling when the other person does). Even if we don't physically do this, we are mirroring it in our head (purple). Finally, we make sense of what is going on and predict what the other person will do going forward given they feel what they feel (orange).

Imagine a scenario where someone comes and asks about marrying their partner. Based on their body language, tone of voice, and frame of the question, you use social perception to gauge their level of happiness with the situation. In the reading, you pull out the Wheel of Fortune card, indicating changes, and as you speak, you can see how their body reaction changes. Even though your interpretation is good, you can feel their body hugging inward and get a sense that they are not open to the idea of marriage. You can then mirror their feelings by experiencing a sense of dread. Then you can mentalize that perhaps they are looking for validation to get out of the situation. As you proceed, your interpretation of the card may also change.

As diviners, we also use the images, charts, or other tools in front of us to help us in this complex process. The entire divination process is a construction of the mental representation of the querent (or even of oneself). We use images, cues, charts, and metaphors to create a narrative that ascribes certain emotional perspectives onto the person. We then contextualize it to the problem at hand and create representations of what the behavior of the person could be, how it would affect them, etc. In many ways, when we lay out the cards, we are walking through the process of social cognition.

STEPS IN UNDERSTANDING THE OTHER

In a reading, when do you recognize emotions in others, at what stage do you empathize by mirroring their emotions, and when do you start contemplating their desires and motivations. This exercise will help you walk through this process and help you breakdown when your own self is intervening in understanding the other.

You will need: Your journal, a writing utensil, a deck of tarot cards, and a friend

Part 1: The Reading

Ask a friend to contemplate on a problem or question. For each of these steps, note down not just your answer but also what you notice about the tone of their question, then layer it with other observations. The exercise starts first with only word cues. Auditory and video cues are subsequently added. Note how each of these is processed.

1. Ask your friend to email or text you their problem or question, then perform the divination.
2. Call them and ask them to state their question, then use your divination method.
3. Video call them or meet them in person to ask the question, then perform the divination.

Part 2: Reflection

1. In each case, ask your friend to state how they "heard" your answer. Were there changes? Did it affect them differently?
2. In each of these cases, how did you mirror or mentalize the other?
3. What was the mental state of your friend?

4. Did you add more adjectives or different adjectives to describe them as you moved through the divination process?
5. Which method of communicating with your friend allowed you to be the best diviner?
6. What cues (posture, word choice, speech, tone) helped you best in your reading?

Contemplate: Do you avoid using certain mediums (texting, calling, video chatting, meeting in person) during your intuitive process? Why or why not?

Musings

The divination process is a transaction and an exercise in social cognition. As social animals, we have learned to understand the emotional state of others so as to best respond to them. We are looking at facial expressions, body postures, tone of voice, and numerous other signals from others in order to decipher what emotional state they are in. As we do this, we tend to mirror their emotional states within ourselves, a means of empathizing with the other, allowing us to feel what they are feeling. We are, at the same time, also creating elaborate pictures in our head of what makes them feel this way. This scene building helps us understand the inner needs and wants of the other person and imagine what their future choices will be. All these elements are put together during a divination session, with the symbols and metaphors of your charts or cards as a means to develop different scenes.

A divination session is not a static event where the diviner says, "This is how it is." Rather, the querent, as they listen to the narratives, look at images, and compare metaphors, comes up with their own mental images of what their options are. In their head, they are picturing their futures—the myriad of possibilities—and developing emotional responses to each of those paths. This adds another layer of dynamism to this transaction.

I hope this section has given you some tools to recognize some of the steps you go through when empathizing with the other and the complex ways in which we delve into the desires and motivations of someone else. It is important to recognize that this ability to mentalize scenes of another is not something innate but something that we train for at a very young age, which means that we all have the power to learn and improve on our abilities to picture future actions of others based on the information that we have.

In the next section, we will venture into the world of prediction, forecasting, and precognition and how neuroscience can inform these topics.

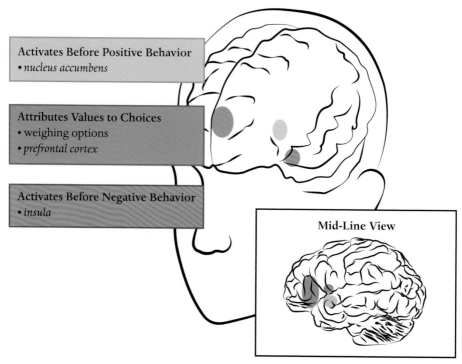

Activates Before Positive Behavior
• *nucleus accumbens*

Attributes Values to Choices
• weighing options
• *prefrontal cortex*

Activates Before Negative Behavior
• *insula*

Mid-Line View

Illustration 12: Anatomy of Prediction and Forecasting

If I split the brain down the midline of the skull, along the nose, we can expose areas that help with the prediction of behavior. Toward the front of the head, behind the third eye, is the medial prefrontal cortex (green), which weighs options by placing values on them. If I draw a string from your ears on each side through your head, we will intersect the nuclear accumbens (blue), which predicts positive behavior (just do it!). Slightly in front of it and further out is the insula (red), which predicts negative behavior (avoidance!).

CHAPTER 5
PREDICTION AND NEUROFORECASTING

O ver the years, we have moved away from thinking of divination as a fore-casting tool and toward seeing it as one to gain deeper understanding of both our choices and ourselves. But it is human nature to contemplate both the past and the future, and there is a sense of excitement in thinking about pre-diction and precognition. Anticipating events and their outcomes is something that is an integral part of our lives—of all animal lives. Our brains are by nature predictive organs. In order to survive, all animals have to anticipate risks, weigh opportunities, and course correct mistakes. At every instance, we all are trying to predict what the next moment will be in order to move appropriately and func-tion in this world. As an example of a simple instance, let us say you are walking down the road. You expect the path to be at a certain level, and this allows you to put your foot forward a certain way, with a certain amount of pressure, with some force so that you can move without falling down. On the other hand, if you were walking up some stairs or an incline, your brain will predict a different need for movement and adjust your muscle efforts accordingly. Small predictions and anticipations allow us to function with ease in the world.

So, why is this important for divination? Even as we lay out cards or the chart, we begin anticipating what symbols will appear and what would lead to what. The narrative threads, next steps, and possible expected outcomes begin to be laid out from the moment the query is posited and sometimes even before by just observing someone, noticing their tone or language. While sometimes these expectation jumps may lead you down the wrong path, in many instances, you may be right on cue—thanks to your past experiences and constant recali-bration of your expectations over time. Even if you were not using divination as a means of foretelling, you are deliberating choices, considering outcomes, and laying out future possibilities.

Anticipation and Expectation

Imagine you are walking down the road toward your coffee shop, and you step on a sharp object, leading you to jump aside. This would be an example of a non-anticipated action. In fact, you anticipated that the path would be clear, which is why you were not looking for something sharp.

Let's say you reach the coffee place. You open the door to the coffee shop and hear a squeak. Every time you open the door, you hear the squeak. So, when you come in the next day and push the door open, your brain is almost waiting, anticipating the squeak even before the sound happens! Anticipation is the brain supposing a certain thing to follow based on patterns that repeated before.

Once you open the squeaky door, the first thing that happens is the barista at the counter greeting you. This is also something that you begin to expect. Your brain is picturing what scenes will happen in the future as you move into the coffee shop. Expectation is the image of what would happen next that is present in the brain. But because our world is not static, our brain constantly reevaluates its prediction, anticipation, and expectation. Next time you walk toward the coffee shop, you will look out for sharp objects, as now your brain anticipates them and has recalibrated how you walk along that particular road.

When you have a series of images (i.e., rose, thorn, rose, thorn, rose …), you begin to anticipate what is going to happen next. You would expect that next in the sequence would be a thorn. We need to be able to anticipate and predict what will happen next so that we can interact with our environment and respond to it in a timely fashion.[43] We can then go beyond immediate expectation to that of what could happen in the future; perhaps you anticipate a bouquet of flowers given all the roses and thorns. You now have a predicted event, and you will then compare what actually happens to what you predicted to see if your expectations were correct or not. If they were, you will now know what to expect better the next time around. If your prediction was incorrect, then you now have to recalibrate your expectations of what these images mean!

---

43. Bubic, von Cramon, and Schubotz, "Prediction, Cognition and the Brain."

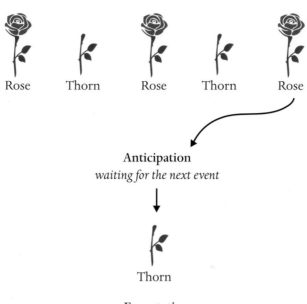

Anticipation
waiting for the next event

Thorn

Expectation
predicting in our minds what will
appear based on our calculations

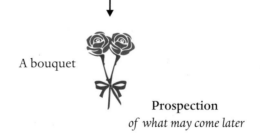

A bouquet

Prospection
of what may come later

Image 23: Expectation and Anticipation

ANTICIPATION AND EXPECTATION

Understanding your sense of anticipation and how much you expect from situations will help you calibrate your foresight.

You will need: Your journal and a writing utensil

1. List the ways in which you anticipate events. Think of small things (e.g., you hear a car, anticipate it coming round the corner, expect to see it, and then see it) and also large things (e.g., your horoscope says you will meet someone special, you encounter someone at a gathering, and you make plans).
2. Think of the times when your anticipation and expectation did not match up. How did you learn from this (e.g., maybe you heard a car, but when you looked did not see one)?

Where Does Anticipation Occur?

As adults we have a lifetime of experiences and baggage, both emotional and physical. This has led us to understand how different situations unfold, how to read people, and how to perceive situations. These millions of instances of choices, ideas, beliefs, and outcomes have calibrated how we will anticipate events or the unfolding of different situations. Each of these is influenced by sensory inputs—what we see, what we hear, what we smell in the current scenario. These serve as the inputs that trigger specific anticipatory ideas in our brain. Our neurons are not just sitting idle all the time. They are constantly trying to see what's going to happen next so that when the event does occur, the circuits needed can spring into action. They are anticipating events, and predicting how the brain will react when they happen.

Many times we smack ourselves on the forehead saying, "I should have known that would happen!" That's remarkable, as right behind the forehead is where neurons activate in a synchronized manner to trigger anticipation (the prefrontal cortex). They are waiting to act a certain way given a certain set of circumstances (prediction). The hope is to reduce the gap between what is predicted and what is actually done. We face this all the time. You may see a cup of coffee and put out your hand to pick it up. Your brain says that if you use this amount of force, the cup can be picked up. But if someone had secretly put a bunch of stones in the cup, it would be way heavier, and you may not be able to move the cup. In this case, what you anticipated and predicted is different from what really happened. So, now you learn. The brain networks being changeable, you now know that not all coffee mugs weigh the same and to anticipate better next time.

This is seen even in physiological responses. If you are shown images of a dot moving at a certain speed across a screen, your visual system tracks the dot as it moves and the neurons light up in a nice serial fashion. After a few minutes of this, if the dot is just shown at the starting point, researchers have found that the brain still lights up in a serial fashion, even though the dot is no longer moving across the screen. Your brain is anticipating this movement and is already programmed to predict that the dot is going to move in a certain manner.[44]

When you see a moving object like a bee or a fly, you expect it to move a certain way and in a certain direction (Image 24). Your brain becomes activated as it moves along a certain trajectory. What is now known is that your brain areas become active even before the insect has moved in a certain way, in a manner predicting what is going to happen next. It is anticipating the event. We rely on such mechanisms constantly during everyday activities such as driving, walking, etc. The brain then compares what happened to what was predicted and makes corrections so that you can react better the next time.

We probably have dealt with this in readings countless times. A card or image or pattern may represent something in many, many readings, but it may have different interpretations when it appears elsewhere. While you are using past experiences to relay a certain narrative with respect to that image, it may be leading you down the wrong path in this current instance. Or you go into the reading anticipating a certain outcome, but the cards or images suggest otherwise. There is then this disconnect where you expected something but were given a different answer. What do you do then? How do you react when your prediction or interpretation does not match with the narrative in front of you?

---

44. Walsh et al., "Evaluating the Neurophysiological Evidence," 242–68.

Visual trajectory

Brain signals following object

A   B   C

Visual object, followed by no movement

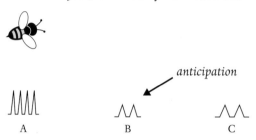

anticipation

A   B   C

Anticipatory brain signals
despite lack of moving object

Image 24: Anticipation of Neurons

Journal Exercise 29
PARSING EXPECTATIONS DURING A READING

Use these questions to parse out when your anticipation and expectations set in during a divination session. Do these initial expectations
stand through the whole reading? Or do they just lay the foundation
for how things will unfold? How do you reconcile if what you expected
was contradictory to what you read in your chart or cards? Do you

retract your initial expectations, or do you fit the symbols into the narrative that you had initially formed?

You will need: Your journal, a writing utensil, and a deck of tarot cards

Part 1: Jumping Ahead in a Reading

1. Shuffle the tarot cards for a minute, and begin the divination process by thinking of a question. How often have you already answered the question in your head before you read the cards (or the chart) in front of you?
2. Do you change your interpretation or mind midway through a reading?
3. Do you ever find a disconnect between what you expected and what you say?
4. Have ever you gone for a reading where you expected the cards to be read a certain way or have a question answered a certain way but had it interpreted differently? How did you react? In these situations, do you figure out why there was a disconnect between what you anticipated and what was said?

Part 2: The Anticipatory Reading

1. Pull out three cards but keep them closed.
2. Open the first card.
3. Write down what you think the second image or theme is going to be. Observe your feelings before opening the card.
4. Open the second card.
5. Write down how you feel when you see this image. Does it match what you said in step 3?
6. Write down what you think the third card or image is going to be. Observe your feelings before opening the card.
7. Open the third card.
8. Write down how you feel when you see this image. Does it match what you said in step 6?

9. Did your "expectation" match the cards you pulled? Why did you have a certain expectation?

Contemplate: In statistics there is the concept of overfitting. It is when we adjust the interpretation of the data to suit our initial ideas/biases. Does the first card in a reading set up a theme that then determines your interpretation of the following cards? Or does your interpretation strictly follow the meanings of the cards? Does a theme ever emerge before you even lay the first card out?

Brain Prediction of Body Reactions

We already spoke in detail about the concept of interoception. We can also look at it this way—as we navigate the world, our brains predict what may happen inside the body based on past experiences. This prediction is the basis for how we experience the world.[45] So, if you touched something for the first time and it burned you, the next time you see this object, the brain anticipates or predicts that your body will be burned. You would then try to avoid it. But maybe the next time the object does not burn. This is termed as a prediction error, and the brain tries to make sense of it. Was something turned on the last time and it was turned off now? This causes the brain to recalibrate how to interact with the object and predict future outcomes. This could then alter the way the body reacts to this object. Maybe you approached it with clenched muscles before and now there is an apparent relaxation in the body? This alters the way we interact with the world. For the most part, we have been told that our perceptions and senses trigger how we act and interact with the world, but actually, how we interact with the world around us alters how we perceive the world.[46]

This happened to me when I was living in Los Angeles. As I walked to the bus stop each morning, I crossed this house with a wire fence. Each time I walked past, this big dog would rush up from the house and bark at me furiously. I have been scared of dogs from a very young age, and somehow dogs seem to sense

45. Barrett and Simmons, "Interoceptive Predictions in the Brain."
46. Bubic, von Cramon, and Schubotz, "Prediction, Cognition and the Brain."

this. Anyhow, I started to expect the barking and crossed the street just before I passed the house. A few weeks later, the dog stopped barking at me, and I started walking by the house again. But one day, just when my guard was down and I started to relax, the dog rushed up and barked, causing me to jump. My brain had been lulled into a certain predictive scenario that the dog was finally used to me, but the dog had a different tactic. It had trained me to become complacent and then startled me.

Journal Exercise 30
RELYING ON BODILY ANTICIPATION

How much do you rely on anticipation for recognizing something? Will your perception of things be altered with new / more information or will it remain the same? This exercise will walk you through some of these ideas.

You will need: Your journal, a writing utensil, a friend, a box (a cardboard box or some other opaque one), and some everyday objects or toys

1. Ask your friend to hide an object in the box.
2. Without looking at the box, put your hand in it and feel the object.
3. Think about how you can use the object and what it looks like.
4. Write down what you think.
5. Pull out the object and see if your perception / expected use of the object is altered.
6. Write down how different your expectation was from the reality.

Contemplate: Does your answer to a querent change as the reading progresses?

Neuroforecasting

The question before us is: Are there instances or evidence of prediction that goes beyond these instinctual responses and short-term predictive adaptations that allow us to regulate our everyday lives? But long-term predictions are part of everyone's life! We prepare for the future. We imagine certain lives for ourselves and then plan for certain things, logical reasoning laying out a flowchart that if we do A, B, and C, we will get result D. And then we move along that course. So, long-term planning is also a part of our brains. Nonhuman animals may even do this instinctually with regards to timing babies for seasonal changes, following migratory paths, listening to their internal clocks and the world around them before the cold sets in.

Scientists are now beginning to explore the field of neuroforecasting—raising the question: Can we actually predict events? This is controversial, but also exciting, and we are at a point in time where we have imaging tools that help us attempt to answer this question. Current experiments revolve around asking people to predict events based on little information and relying entirely on their intuition. The questions posed are similar to "Which songs will be the most popular in six months?" and "Which products will be bestsellers in a year?" Brain recordings of individuals are then made while they make their choice. In many instances, it was found that while people consciously indicated that they preferred song A or item V, their brain activation patterns revealed that intuitively they anticipated that song D or item X would be the most popular! There was an unconscious activation in their brains that pointed to a positive predictive outcome.[47]

So, how is this possible? It is likely that, as we mentioned before, we are taking in different bits and pieces of information and our unconscious brain is able to parse them out into a certain outcome. Even if logical reasoning points to a different outcome, we are able to anticipate or predict what the correct trend is going to be ahead of time. The exciting part here is that a collective group of people can accurately predict what could happen and that most of the time, this is hidden inside our unconscious.

Neural activity in the brain predicts choices such as purchasing and risk-taking behaviors. Choosing positive choices or behaviors (buy this, do that, etc.)

---

47. Knutson and Genevsky, "Neuroforecasting Aggregate Choice," 110–15.

activates the nucleus accumbens.[48] If I split your brain right down the middle vertically (down the forehead, nose, and chin) and track a line from the bottom of your ears to the middle of the brain, that is approximately where you would see the nucleus accumbens. The medial prefrontal cortex in the front of the brain is where you weigh the value of different choices and aggregate them. Activity in these two areas seem to predict how you are going to react to a particular decision (Illustration 12). Will you choose A or B? Nucleus accumbens activation predicted what will be downloaded on the internet two years later! While these brain areas predicted positive behavior, the insula and the amygdala predicted avoidance behaviors (why you ran away from something or did not like a particular object).

Moving from this level of unconscious decision-making to the point of individual action takes many steps and many brain layers. And by the time you move from what your unconscious mind suggests to actually making the choice, it may change! This is why even if you know something deep down, you may consciously act very differently, as the logical mind may override your unconscious choices. But it also suggests that even before you take action, you may have made an unconscious choice to act a certain way before you have consciously executed that action. And by looking at your activity in the nucleus accumbens, mPFC, and insula, we should be able to know what your individual choices are—perhaps long before you have made the conscious choice.

The exciting part about using tarot or other divination tools is that we can perhaps open a window into this unconscious, creating a way for us to take a peek within to try to figure out what decisions we have made but are not yet aware of. So even though the conscious mind is troubled by the lack of resolution or a decision, we can use these images or other tools as conduits to help us understand what we are planning deep inside.[49]

---

48. Knutson and Greer, "Anticipatory Affect," 3771–86.
49. Knutson and Genevsky, "Neuroforecasting Aggregate Choice."

Journal Exercise 31
MAKING PREDICTIONS

Figuring out how your brain navigates forecasting can help you understand the processes, how you attribute values to different choices (using the medial prefrontal cortex), and what kinds of choices you avoid (insula) or act on (nucleus accumbens). These questions will also give you insight on groupthink and how the collective can sometimes predict outcomes better than an individual.

You will need: Your journal, writing utensil, a deck of tarot cards, and four to five friends

Part 1: Forecasting the Future
1. Think of a situation or problem that will be resolved three to six months from now that you do not yet know the resolution of.
2. Write down how you anticipate the situation will be resolved.
3. Now pick a card or two to glean what the outcome will be. In your journal, note down the cards.
4. Think of the situation or problem from step 1.
5. Ask your friends how they think this situation will be resolved.
6. Ask them to pull one or two tarot cards to answer the question and write down their quick immediate thoughts/insight from their cards.
7. Compare notes between your journal entry and your friends' answers.
8. Is the behavior/choice a positive one or one of avoidance?
9. What values do you attribute to the choice at hand to resolve the issue.

Part 2: Revisiting in Six Months
1. Look back on your answers to the situation.
2. What was the outcome?
3. Did you manage to predict the outcome?

4. Was the crowd-sourced solution/prediction more accurate?
5. Would you interpret your cards differently now that you know the outcome?

Precognition

Precognition is different from prediction. This is when you are able to provide information about a future event that you had no way of knowing or inferring. Imagine a situation where you listen to ten songs and are asked which ones will be the most popular in a year. There you have some information to act on. Your brain can process a tune, knows pop or rock, and uses some data to make some predictions. On the other hand, think of a situation where you suddenly blurt out "Valdez Rules," and six months down the line, the most popular tune is a song previously unheard called "Valdez Rules." This would be the difference between prediction and precognition.

This is met with significant skepticism from the scientific community (and rightly so, as many claims are indeed far-fetched). However, there have been some controversial studies where the participants' future knowledge influenced past performance. Many of these ideas are difficult to even process, as they break fundamental laws of physics and thermodynamics. There have been some theories of retro-causal effects (the future influencing the past) rooted in quantum mechanics.[50] One problem in tackling such questions is the inherent bias of the experimenters (whether they believe in precognition or not), which can influence the outcomes or interpretation of the experiment. But with more sophisticated technologies being developed for neuroscience, maybe it is only a matter of time until such questions can be experimentally tested.

Studies show that one's belief in precognition or the prediction of the future is linked to the level of control one has in their life.[51] The lesser the control, the stronger the belief in precognition, psychics, etc. On some level, the prediction of the future gives a person more control over their choices. Most tarot, oracle, or astrology readings do not involve grand predictions. Instead, many of them

---

50. Bem, "Feeling the Future," 407–25.
51. Greenaway, Louis, and Horney, "Loss of Control Increases Belief."

suggest probabilities, potentials, and paths with certain outcomes highlighted. Of course, one can claim these to be vague (with the listener allowed to fit them within their own scenario) or apt (with the cards pointing exactly in the right direction). Many of these are transactional analyses between the reader and the questioner. That is, the listener is going to take away whatever they heard from the reading. They construct their own future scenarios in their heads and may thus "confirm" what fits their best inner narrative to be true.

So how can your brain hold multiple possibilities and multiple future outcomes at the same time in order to help resolve situations? One way of trying to explain this is using quantum mechanics, which includes precognition.[52] Quantum mechanics allows for phenomena such as superposition and entanglement, which can work on the scales of atoms and subatomic particles. This could be the basis of quantum cognition. While the scale of the brain is quite large, at its core, your brain is just a composite of neurons, and these neurons themselves are just a conglomerate of protein channels, fats (lipids), and ionic movement. Instead of us examining the brain as a physical entity, if we begin looking at it as an electromagnetic wave generator, we could perhaps better contemplate consciousness and how we perceive the "waves of others" or even the "waves of the universe." Indeed, this transcendence from being individuals to being "merged" with the universal energy has been propounded by mystics in different religions and also patients who are experiencing strokes—where the divide between the physical plane with discrete forms subsides and melds into a larger consciousness. At the moment, we do not have the tools or the capacity to investigate these ideas.

Journal Exercise 32
YOUR PREDICTIVE BRAIN

Trying to understand the ability to predict is fraught, but journaling about questions may help you walk through the process.

You will need: Your journal and a writing utensil

---

52. Taylor, "The Nature of Precognition," 19–38.

1. Think of a time when you predicted something. What was the logical progression for that prediction?
2. Can you think of an event where the collective conscious around you was aware that something was going to work out?

Musings

At the moment of this writing, neuroscience as a field is delving into exciting areas such as forecasting and precognition. The tools for brain imaging and simultaneous imaging of multiple people are being developed and are becoming more sophisticated. Also, more scientists are becoming open to exploring ideas that would have been anathema a decade or so back. Concepts that were considered esoteric or taboo are becoming more mainstream. Even phenomena such as mindfulness and meditation were not part of experimental paradigms a few decades ago, and now there are a lot of studies involving these practices. Some of this is because scientists themselves are beginning to practice some of these exercises, thereby removing the bias barriers toward them.

In many ways, our questions about the brain and what it is capable of doing are restricted by the technology we have to explore it. We are also limited by our own sensory systems—our senses of sight, hearing, smell, touch, and taste are the primary ways in which we can observe the brain and its functions. There is an added element of confounding in that the object of study (the brain) is also the instrument used to observe and analyze it. The hope is that we will be able to overcome some of these limitations with new approaches and technologies to observe brain activity and functions.

It is always exciting to think that you can glimpse into the future. I hope this chapter gave you a sense of what is known about the predictive brain—from an everyday life-anticipation standpoint, as well as moving into the forecasting aspects. As the field of neuroscience progresses, I foresee (pun intended) more experiments that will address these questions of forecasting, prediction, and precognition. As we talk about these topics, I do have to add the caveat that charlatans and practitioners of bad faith exist in the field of divination—and they have the ability to cause a lot of harm. In many ways, science has been used as an instrument to debunk many of these bad elements. Perhaps science can become the tool in the future to observe some of these processes of divination and help us understand them further.

CHAPTER 6
TAROT AND NEUROSCIENCE: SPREADS AND CORRESPONDENCES

W e have spoken a lot about how neuroscience is connected to the interpretation of tarot and divination symbology. Can we use tarot spreads to delve deeper into our own brains? In this chapter, we use some popular spreads and create some new ones to help you explore more of your brain.

The Celtic Cross Spread: From Brain to Action

The Celtic cross spread is a popular tarot spread that involves ten cards. There are two cards representing the questioner, and the next four cards deal with both internal and external influences, which together represent the current situation. The final four cards deal with outside inputs and how you can use or overcome them to get to a specific outcome. I think of a Neuro Tarot modification of the Celtic cross as a brain and spinal cord spread. You can be within the brain and have all the thoughts and ideas in the world, but to spring to action and execute them, you need the spinal cord. So together, these cards represent the movement of thinking to action, a shift from internal to external. Both are essential, a combination of Shiva and Shakti.

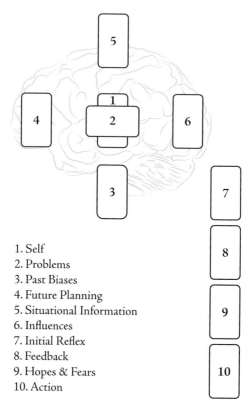

1. Self
2. Problems
3. Past Biases
4. Future Planning
5. Situational Information
6. Influences
7. Initial Reflex
8. Feedback
9. Hopes & Fears
10. Action

Image 25: Celtic Cross and the Self

1. The Self: Used to represent the current state of mind of the questioner; a snapshot of who you are at this current moment in time. This would fall deep within the brain, the *insula*, which is thought to be the seat of consciousness.

2. The Problem: Your questions, desires, issues, and problems that arise out of this internal state (or in conflict with it). One helpful aspect of a reading is that it allows you to put your question into words, moving it from an abstract idea to conscious thought, linking between different brain areas.

3. Past Biases: Your current actions will be influenced by the past, as we have a constantly learning brain that recalibrates. Inhibitions are learned to modulate future behaviors. The *temporal lobe* is the repository of long-term memories, integrating them with emotional information from the amygdala. This is also the seat of your unconscious biases.

4. Future Planning: Your actions are also influenced by what you think the out-come will be. Expectations. This leads to planned action and visualization of how the scenario will unfold. The *premotor area of the forebrain* and the default mode network rules pre-action planning.

5. Taking Stock (Situational Information): The *parietal lobe* takes in all the sensory information available, including body positioning (proprioception) and sense of space. Integrating all the sensory information, you can then think of how best to move forward toward the goal.

6. Influences (External and Internal Information): While you may have all the ideas planned out, new information is constantly entering into the brain via the eyes, the ears, smell, touch, etc. The *midbrain*, with the *colliculi*, creates a map of the world around us using both auditory and visual information. You respond to situations with external sensory processing, as well as with internal mental imagery and visualizations from associations.

Now that you have taken stock of the situation, how will you move forward?

7. Initial Reflex/Control: Your cranial nerves originating in the *hind brain* allow you to execute actions without thinking about all the other "regular" functions, like breathing, temperature, eye movements, etc. It's a well-oiled machine that can run on its own. Yet, it is influenced by fears, hopes, and other such inputs. How you react is both primal and learned.

8. Feedback/Sensation: As you move forward with actions, you interact with the world and draw in information through your body. Texture, heat, pain—all of this is delivered to you via the *dorsal root ganglion* into the spinal cord (and then to the brain). Responses to these inputs are quick reflexes or more nuanced. Sometimes you step on a thorn and quickly withdraw in sharp pain, but if you know the alternative is worse, you would accept it and move on.

9. Hopes and Fears: While it is easy to think of oneself as a machine, we are influenced by hormones coursing through us that modulate our actions. How we respond to stress is shaped within the womb. It is not good or bad, but we have to recognize that our emotions do shape our actions. Knowing why you

feel the way you do may help. Take a deep breath, think of your hormones in balance (*your* hypothalamus), and move forward.

10. Action/Outcomes: When neurons talk to muscles, action becomes external. Thought is allowed to play in the physical world. Acetylcholine is the chemical that communicates between your nerve cells and the muscle cells. You have all the information, have recalibrated, assessed, and overcome fears—now the work is to be done; don't worry about the outcome.

Self and the Other Spread

This spread shows you how you relate as a reader to your querent—how you define your own self and see the other with empathy. How do you mirror the other person's emotions and what can you predict about the other person's behavior? This spread would overlay a regular spread where you have laid out what course of action a person would take. It is to add further clarity either regarding their choices or your interpretation of the regular spread.

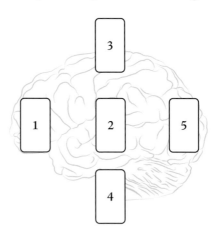

1. Your Inner Self
2. Empathy for Others
3. Mirroring the Other in You
4. Understanding Others' Actions
5. Future Prognostications

Image 26: Self and the Other Spread

1. Your Inner Self: Where you are emotionally at this point in the reading. The default mode network and the *orbitofrontal cortex* can indicate where your current mental state is.

2. Empathy for the Other: How you perceive the other and recognize their emotions. Are you able to perceive their emotions? The area just above your ears (*temporoparietal junction*) plays a part in this.

3. Mirroring the Other in You: Part of empathy is how you would feel if you were in the other person's shoes. Mirroring activates parts that make you feel what they feel. This is perceived along the crown of your head in the *parietal lobe*.

4. Understanding the Other's Actions: Your understanding of their actions and motivations. Here is where you can contemplate their desires, influences, and choice making. Brush your hand behind the top of your ears. This area (the *superior temporal sulcus*) is activated in this mentalizing process.

5. Future Prognostications: What can they do to resolve the situation. Based on the cards above, you can provide context to talk about next steps and their ramifications.

Narrative Arc Spread

The narrative arc spread walks you through the process of plot formation with a question, potential roadblocks or discordance, which the querent might find difficult to process, and finally the possibilities for the future. This spread would be especially useful when dealing with a querent who has come in with preconceived outcomes, or when you feel stuck in a loop regarding your choices.

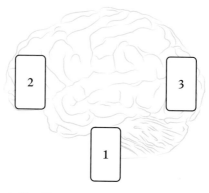

1. Plot Narrative
2. Roadblocks to Acceptance
3. Future Contemplation

Image 27: The Narrative Arc Spread

1. **Plot Narrative:** When you, as a diviner, are giving a card reading (or interpreting a chart), a story begins to form. This card can represent the reading. The *temporal lobe* is involved in the making of this narrative.

2. **Roadblocks to Acceptance:** However, the querent may not be ready to hear what you say or may find the information discordant to their own expectations. You can elucidate these roadblocks to acceptance. This card can represent these roadblocks. It may be interesting to ask your querent to interpret this card.

3. **Future Contemplation:** Thinking about the future is a part of the *default mode network*, which sets up how things unfold with different choices. This card is a view into the querent's crossroads.

Journal Exercise 33
THE ANTICIPATION SPREAD

Use this spread to overcome the bias of expectation and open to newer inputs. Alternatively, you can use this spread to set intentions.

1. Pull out three cards but keep them closed.
2. Open the first card.
3. Write down what you expect the second image or theme is going to be.
4. Ask the querent to write down what they want or expect the next image to be about.
5. Open the second card.
6. Write down how you feel when you see this image. Does it match what you said in step 3?
7. Ask the querent how they feel about the second image and if it matches their expectation.
8. Write down what the third card or image is going to be. Also observe what your feelings are before opening the card.
9. Ask the querent to write down what they want or expect the next image to be about.
10. Open the third card.
11. Write down how you feel when you see this image. Does it match what you said in step 8?
12. Ask the querent how they feel about the third image and if it matches their expectation.

Tarot Correspondences with Neuroscience

Tarot has a lot of correspondences. For centuries, folks have associated the symbology with the Kabbalah, with the zodiac, with numerology, with deities across religions, and more. To me, tarot being a window into our mind and the brain being the main interpreter of the cards, it felt like there should be natural correspondences with the world of neuroscience. This was in essence my main foray to create the Neuro Tarot deck. Below I delve into the major arcana and its relations to the neuroscience.

0. The Fool: The Fool constitutes beginnings and resembles the phenomenon of *neurulation*, when neurons are born, but with no specific identity and can wander making connections, exploring their full potential in the future.

1. The Magician: The Magician follows the Fool and has all the agency to take action and move things forward. Every action we take—every breath, each thought—is a product of signals that cascade through neurons called *action potentials*. These are essential for every function in us and are fundamental energy.

2. The High Priestess: The High Priestess asks you to retreat within yourself for a period of self-examination. Meditation and contemplation can reveal more than an external quest for knowledge. Think of the contemplative mind and the messages that you store inside of yourself. Situated right above the third ventricle (one of the cavities within the brain), the *pineal gland* is able to secrete hormones into the cerebrospinal fluid and into the blood stream. One of these hormones, melatonin, serves as a homing signal in animals, guiding them back home. Dwell on this to find your own place, your own home, by reaching within.

3. The Empress: The *pituitary* is the seat of hormonal control and homeostasis. From regulating hunger, desire, and temperature to fertility and puberty, it is the seat of holistic regulation. When you think about the Empress and all her bounty and plenty, think of the pituitary deep within and the hormones it releases to make you feel all the different emotions—hunger, lust, contentment, and more.

4. The Emperor: While thoughts flow like rivers, bursting through the mind, the *frontal lobe* exerts control and inhibition to regulate them and allow for our humanness to emerge. Without this, we would be wandering only on instincts and have no conscious creation. Think of the frontal lobe, bulging forward above your eyes, and how it serves as the Emperor of your thoughts and actions, bringing stability, authority, and control.

5. The Hierophant: The *hippocampus* is the seat of memory. Described as resembling a seahorse or a ram's horn, it is here that scientists search for the clues for the storehouse of knowledge. Time, distance, and location are also encoded in this area of the brain. In some ways, the lesson may be use it or lose it—things can be learned, expertise can be achieved. When you meditate on the Hierophant and all his expertise, guidance, and the power of knowledge, think of the hippocampus.

6. The Lovers: *Oxytocin*, called the "love hormone" has been associated with pair bonding and monogamy in animals and also with maternal/paternal connections and behaviors. Embrace the bonding, share your hearth, feel the resonance in the other, filling you with abundance with the help of the hypothalamus. Embrace the relationships and all the ramifications that ensue with the Lovers.

7. The Chariot: The *Chariot* points to overcoming obstacles and responding to situations presented with appropriate control and confidence. Life is full of choices—should I stay or should I go—and the most primal among them is that of "fight or flight." The *adrenal glands* situated atop the kidneys respond to stress signals from the brain and release adrenaline and cortisol, which then prompts action. The adrenal glands may be situated quite afar from the brain, but are still under the control of *neuro-hormonal* control. How one responds to cortisol in different situations may depend on stress receptors in the brain, which are primed in the embryo. The beauty of most biological systems is their self-regulatory aspect—cortisol from the adrenals feedback to the brain to reduce the activation of the stress pathway (it's as if water flowing from a tap closing the faucet). So when you think about making those choices, listen to your body as well.

8. Strength: The core support of neurons is provided by a skeleton structure of *microtubules* that extend everywhere within the neural cell. The shape and integrity of the cell, and hence its function, are supported by these scaffolds. New neuron outgrowth is also extended through these microtubules—exemplifying that strength is not just for sustenance but also growth. When you meditate on the Strength card, the perseverance and self-belief, think of the building blocks, the little bits and pieces, that make you. For if the foundation is not strong, the

structure is weak. It also means that when you feel you don't have strength, start small and build up!

9. The Hermit: Sometimes one needs to withdraw and meditate in order to contemplate on the situation, and this is signified by the solitary Hermit. The *insula* deep in the brain is thought to be the seat of consciousness, and its structure has been shown to be influenced by meditative practices. Imaging studies have revealed connections from the insula to cognitive control processes and affective emotional centers in the limbic system, as well as *sensorimotor* connections. Thus, it serves as a hub for integrating different information with cognitive functioning. It is now thought to be the seat of consciousness.

10. The Wheel of Fortune: How does the brain develop specific regions with specific functions? How does a neural tube transform into a nervous system with a forebrain, motor and sensory neurons, and other parts? *Hox genes* create a milieu of chemicals that diffuse across the embryo, pushing them toward forming different structures. Timing is essential. In many ways, the *Hox genes* embody this meaning of chance and possibilities to the fullest. The *Hox genes* are the ones that shape us into specific entities, creating a chemical soup that molds the embryo over time. Think about all the things that needed to have happened to get you to this moment. Think about the genetic games of chance that led to create you as this perfect creature. You are a living embodiment of the Wheel of Fortune.

11. Justice: To swing between the trees, one needs impeccable balance. This is something that needs to be developed—sometimes beginning as a child. The *cerebellum*, toward the rear of the brain, maintains this functionality, ensuring that we learn patterns so we can swing freely, navigating the world without slipping. When you think of cause and effect—and of gaining a sense of justice—remember that a lot of your own balance was learned and accrued over time.

12. Hanged Man: The *amygdala*, coiled deep within like a serpent, can sometimes trap us with fearful emotions, rendering us paralyzed and confused. Sometimes what we may need is a new perspective to break out of this cycle—one that moves us from the darkness into light. A lot about the Hanged Man is about taking a new perspective and changing. The world looks completely different upside down, so why not take a peek? That way, if you feel stuck and

anxious about a situation, you can find new solutions. Some of our fears are instinctual, calling back to our evolutionary history. The Hanged Man has doubts but also the resources to break free of these chains. Remember to be gentle with yourself, as some of these fears are embodied.

13. Death: When neurons die, they undergo a very systematic process of degeneration. Debris is collected so materials can be reused and also to clear the way for new growth that can follow. Numerous other cells attend the funereal reclamation of the dead neural debris. While Death can mean an end, it also signifies the beginnings of a new cycle. What can be salvaged can be repurposed.

14. Temperance: The *suprachiasmatic nucleus*, situated above the intersection of optic nerves, controls our biorhythm. With the rise and ebb of different hormones and genes, the clocks in our bodies tick. Temperance reminds us that patience is indeed a virtue as even our own bodies have rhythms, with some things cresting at certain times while others follow. Everything is a cycle. We have different body clocks for different organs, but the master clock that coordinates them lies above the optic chasm (where the optic nerves cross each other). In the suprachiasmatic nucleus, there are around twenty thousand autonomous neural oscillators, which are coupled through chemical signals. Remember that everything has its own time and cycles.

15. The Devil: Within all of us are impulses that—when let loose—control us like a puppet, bringing out the devil in us. Without control, we would be puppets played by our uninhibited brain. Baser impulses without reason can indeed lead to hedonism. A lot of impulsivity has to do with inhibition, or lack thereof. The prefrontal cortex and the *basal ganglia* are important in the impulse-control pathway, and damage to these areas leads to an uptick in uncontrolled hedonistic behaviors. These structures are also involved in the risk-reward pathways, thereby tying behaviors with "pleasure."

16. The Tower: Change is the only constant, and our brains are plastic entities that change constantly. Neural connections are formed, then revised, and especially when facing large, emotionally charged events, the brain undergoes rapid changes to adapt and survive. Some of these, one can recover from; others set us on a new path. The Tower reminds us that while changes may be hidden

and beyond our control, the only way is forward—adapt and survive. We experience neural plasticity constantly. This is also the basis of recovery from injury, development from embryo to adulthood, learning new languages, etc. Unforeseen circumstances may alter our functioning and change the way we think drastically because they cause new links within our brain structures. In many ways, this is hopeful, as it shows that nothing is set in stone. It can be altered.

17. The Star: Neurons have the capacity to *regenerate* and are pretty creative in trying to forge paths forward. Many times, they have to find ways around scar tissue or other barriers and jump across to reestablish connections with their targets. When one path of escape breaks, look for another. This is the essence of the hope signified by the Star.

18. The Moon: While it appears that you are in control, most of your functions are unseen, running on some innate signals—seamlessly. Follow their lead. The brain stem has program generators that can control many unconscious functions of the body. These are essential, innate acts, such as heartbeat regulation, digestion, breathing, swallowing, etc. It is also the center for moods, sleep, arousal, and wakefulness. Recent studies have shown that mindfulness meditation improves the quality of the brain stem gray matter and this correlated with an increased feeling of positive well-being. While the moon may be nebulous, she is also instinctual and embodied. Listen to your inner signs.

19. The Sun: Dance across the universe with gratitude, consciously recognizing the positives and creating your own happiness. The study of happiness has been elusive—some talk about reward seeking, others about misery fleeing and recently identified centers of gratitude. The *nucleus accumbens*, prefrontal cortex, and the ventral tegmental area, which form a network of neural centers, are all implicated in feeling happiness and tying it with emotion. These are tied together by a circuit called the *medial forebrain bundle*. Endorphins, which target native opiate receptors in the brain, are released when we experience stimuli like laughing, touching, singing, and smiling and sensations like orgasms. All these trigger the happiness circuits. There also seems to be a difference in the left and right brains in the happiness circuitry—with the left frontal lobe being activated during meditation and laughter. Also, different individuals have

different baselines of happiness, which may have some genetic basis. Research also alludes to the fact that pushing away negative thoughts may not be enough to become happy. There is a greater likelihood of triggering happiness centers through processes like mediation or through sensations of touch, sound, taste, etc.

20. Judgement: In Judgement, resolution arises from reflecting on all sides and collating the information. Like a butterfly needs both wings to fly freely, we need both sides of the brain to function well. The *corpus callosum* is a tract of fibers that joins the two cerebral hemispheres, integrating information between them. Also referred to as the commissure, the corpus callosum serves to communicate and integrate sensory/motor information as well as cognitive function between the two hemispheres.

21. The World: Even the smallest drop of water can encompass an ocean with its power of regeneration and collection. *Neural stem cells* have the ability to be altered into numerous different futures. Once they are set on a path, they then differentiate to achieve a specific structure and function. This gives them a certain purpose, which could be to send or receive information, to integrate signals, or to offer support. They are also used to help with recovering from injury and with the constant changes in adulthood. In many ways, the stem cells offer a view of all that can be, but with the power to regenerate, they also can replenish the pool. Like the World, they serve as a complete cycle, encompassing one and all.

The Minor Arcana

How do we parlay the suits into the world of Neuro Tarot? One way to think about it is to think of the elements—air, water, earth, and fire—and how they relate to the world of brains. Looking into the world of tarot decks, many are inspired by animals (cats, dogs, animal spirits), moving us away from an anthropocentric viewpoint. Our brains and what we know about them exists only because of all the creatures that came before us—because of how they contributed to the knowledge as experimental subjects and also by way of evolution. In essence, we have the blueprints of millions of creatures encoded within us.

I imagine the suit of cups to be Molluska—snails, clams, and mussels—with their cornucopia of shells that bask in the mysteries of water, but also octopus and squid, the masters of illusion, predation, and camouflage, the epitome of mystery, desire, and control. Molluscs have taught us so much about neuroscience, from memory systems to feeding systems to understanding complex behaviors.

The pentacles are earthy and material, bringing to mind burrowing, walking on solid ground, and trees. For me, the pentacles are Mammalia. Mammals are abundant on the soil, from voles and rabbits to rats and monkeys. Materialism also invokes objects like fur, pelts, and other rich fabrics often derived from mammals. They also represent, in a way, where a lot of research money is devoted. Here, neuroscience research uses these creatures more as scientific tools rather than observing them with a naturalist's curiosity. Brain research into mammals has also yielded some of the most formidable material products—medicines, neurotechnologies, and drugs.

Swords represent air in some elemental correspondences, and I like to envision swords as striking talons or sharp beaks—the suit of Aves. Birds are constantly moving, building, seeking, hunting. But they also suddenly disappear like the wind. Birds have been used in brain research for so long, from Skinner's pigeons learning in boxes to understanding mating rituals to auditory navigation in owls to singing in zebra finches to the fascinating toolmaking in crows. Birds' remarkable behaviors in mating, nesting, and migrating thousands of miles has us contemplating intricate narratives.

Wands are fire in some correspondences. Wands are energy and creativity. They also signify passion. I think of Insecta burrowing into the hot ground with their myriad of tricks to form cooperative colonies, build intricate tunnels, and even survive devastating forest fires. Symbolically insects have been used to represent passion, spirituality, and intuition in different cultures. Scientists have spent countless hours investigating the behaviors of bees and ants, the strategies of praying mantises, and the actions of nimble cockroaches.

Musings

While these correspondences may be tenuous to some, I hope to investigate them further and explore how individual cards can be interpreted within the suits as well. We have a lot to learn from the brains of creatures around us, and we can use that knowledge in our own divination process.

CONCLUSION
YOUR DIVINING BRAIN

Taking a peek into our brains is an exciting journey, and we can use different divination tools to gain access to those thoughts that are locked or deep within us and to things that we don't immediately understand. For some of us, these tools may be looking at clouds, ruminating on tarot cards, consulting with oracles, or looking at planetary alignments. These auguries spark something in us that then percolates and bubbles forth as intuitive insights into our lives and choices. This allows us to create a dialog with our inner selves, forming a sort of language to communicate with that which cannot be verbalized. This is what makes the divination process so magical and exciting. It opens so many doors into realms and delves into our consciousness, making us wonder, "Wow! I thought of that?" or "How did I know that could happen?" and so on.

Throughout this book, we have walked through numerous exercises that have hopefully given you ways to tune up your insightful brain, become better at your intuitive processes, recognize emotions, and listen to your body. These tools need not just be used during the divination process; they can be useful for everyday life. We use intuition and gain insight from all our choices and behaviors, and working through these exercises is a way to systematically become better at this process. The brain, like your body, needs to be exercised, and these tasks presented can help you with that. I would recommend putting a date on your notes and revisiting them after a few months to check if things have changed.

Retraining Your Mind's Eye

We started this book by looking at how we perceive the world, the visual machinery that allows us to interact with things around us, and how that information is broken down and stored. From there we began the elaborate process of building our vision. First, we remade the image, then we added information that allowed us to recognize the image and place it in context. Following this, we textured this mental image with meanings, associations from memories, and then narratives. Our brains are the greatest storytellers and everything is a story that fits into patterns or themes. We use our mental images and memories to form these stories. This is why divination tools like tarot cards and charts are rife with metaphors. We are constantly creating a world of metaphors to try to understand how we fit into it.

While most of us are visual creatures, there may be those among us who are more attuned to other senses—smell, hearing, taste, or touch. Some of us have vivid mental imagery, where beach scenes are picturesque with aqua waves, golden sand, and sparkling seashells. Others can only see a few words or a hint of sketches of waves on the shore in the mind's eye. We talked about how to find out what kind of visualizer you are, how to zero in on your mental imagery, and how to pay attention to how you add meanings and associations to your images.

Do remember that we are human animals. We have a history, a lifetime of experience that has led us to this moment in time, and for all our meditations and hopes of transcendence, we are emotional creatures. How these emotions color your observation of different objects in front of you is also part of the context of any reading. Each of us sees a different version of the same auguries. We use different words to describe them, and we have our own biases in how we interpret the signs. Learn how to identify your main biases, your go-to crutches and meanings. See if they are always right or a habit to be reconsidered. Recognize how you observe, what you observe, and if you can train your eyes to "notice" new things in the patterns in front of you.

Mastering Your Intuition

We now have a story laid in front of us and are on the verge of interpreting it. For many novice readers, the art of interpretation or deriving meaning from divination tools is a step-by-step process of applying what's been learned from books. If this happens, then that is bound to follow—and so on. These novice interpretations are simpler intuitive thoughts that rely on fewer parts of our brain, using mainly our memory systems and current emotional states. However, the leaps of intuition that an expert diviner has are quicker and may not take the logical path, years of experience adding layers of nuance to how they see the auguries in front of them. These intuitions involve more complex brain processes, which are finally integrated in the cingulate cortex to come up with more complex thoughts. Like an expert surgeon cutting blind or a great athlete anticipating the next ball, these expert diviners are going beyond logic to arrive at deep conclusions of how the narrative unfolds and what it means. If you were to ask how you can improve your intuition, the quick answer would be: Practice! Practice! Practice!

Making a call based on intuition does not always mean making the right call! While intuitive decisions are quick and provide us with a resolution at the moment, things don't always turn out to be what we expect. This concept of making intuitive leaps that set your mind at rest is called cognitive ease. Reflecting back on these intuitive decisions, you can wonder why you made the choice you did, why you interpreted things a certain way, or why you thought that the cards meant what you thought. This process of looking back on your intuitive choices after the fact can help you gain insight, learn about your intuitive process, and become better at it. Gaining insight is not easy. A lot of times, we have made the intuitive leaps blind, and there were no conscious signs pointing to what made you move a certain way. Sometimes this insight comes from a logical step-by-step dissection of what we observed, what meanings we used, what patterns we detected, and then the final interpretation we made. But sometimes insight comes to us out of the blue, while in the shower or maybe during a long walk. The hope is to get you to recognize your own abilities, and train yourself to gain insight, thereby improving your intuition going forward.

The reflective (insight) and reflexive (intuition) parts of the brain are very different. But both are essential parts of the divination process. The default mode network, which is responsible for the sense of self, is the one that is implicated in insight processing—almost hinting at the concept of self-realization of the unconscious. Our brain has strategies in place to make sure we can make split-second choices and decisions without needing too much input. At the same time, we have the capacity to store and sift through a wealth of information quickly. Most of this happens deep in the unconscious. It slowly surfaces but sometimes emerges rapidly when we get those deep insights. The exercises to hone your intuition and insight can be visited repeatedly—and will help you get better at making more accurate leaps of faith over time.

Believe In Your Body

None of our thoughts happen in a vacuum, and the fact is we have emotions that are going to offer a different lens to whatever we do. If you are agitated or angry and attempt an intuitive reading, you may interpret the signs in front of you very differently than if you were happy or excited. While we cannot always be a calm, serene soul, we can employ strategies to control our emotional lens prior to a divination so as to be a bit more unbiased in our interpretations. Here it is important to note that most emotions are interpretations of bodily reactions by the brain. Termed interoception, it is another sense that we have; it is the processing of internal body cues from our gut, our heart, our muscles, and other organs. These are then calibrated by our brain to mean one thing or the other. These emotions result in activations or deactivations in the brain. Take a moment to notice if you associate some aspects of your divination tool (tarot cards, chart patterns, etc.) to represent certain emotions.

Given that we are not just our brain but an embodied creature, we should also pause and notice where in our body we feel activated or deactivated when we experience different emotional states. These sensations are then taken to the insula, the amygdala, the prefrontal cortex, and the nucleus accumbens to provide your emotional core affects. From there, we have to then conceptualize that this is indeed the emotion. We match it up with what we felt before to identify the actual emotion. For example, if my body is cold in my feet, hot in my chest, and calm in my arms, that means that I am nervous—or some such. Finally, we verbalize the emotion by attaching words, labels, and meaning to it.

Different cards may hold different emotional valences for us or may make us feel different things in our body. Notice these differences and see if they color your readings. As social creatures, we are also susceptible to the emotions of others. If you are reading for someone else, make sure you are neutral and to ground yourself from being affected by the querent as well. There are strategies by which we can alter our body poses to alter our emotional state. Mindful meditation (or performing some similar ritual) prior to your readings is a great idea. Another important aspect here is that the querent may not be open to your interpretations of the imagery. You can also provide them with some exercises to be more open and accepting of the session. Use the body charts to find out where you feel things, to become more aware of your instinctual reactions. A lot of us use the "gut checks" and body triggers unconsciously during a reading. While

I am not suggesting that you remove the spontaneity from your practice, I do think it might be beneficial for us to notice the cues we use to make those intuitive leaps. And a lot of it comes from the body.

Divining the Other

Most divination does not happen in isolation and usually involves a pair—a questioner and a reader. In such readings, the diviner is constantly engaging in empathizing with the querent, mirroring their emotions and trying to create mental possibilities of their choices and behavior. Humans, as social animals, have the capacity to engage in such cognitive empathy where we try to figure out intentions, desires, and motivations of people around us. The diviner uses this information through the lens of their cards or charts to create a narrative. This narrative has a plot—a beginning, a middle, and a resolution of sorts—or perhaps a multitude of choices that are laid out for the questioner. But as we know, we all hear what we want to hear.

In this dance of divination, the story laid out in front of the questioner is filtered through their own emotional brain. They create their own multitude of future scenes and play them out. Sometimes they may not agree with what is said, causing dissonance. If you are a diviner, keep that in mind. The castles you build from the charts or cards in front of you are ephemeral castles in the clouds or sand. Even as you create them, or even before you create them, the questioner in front of you is dismantling them grain by grain to create their own versions and exploring what best suits their own inner mentalizing process at that moment in time. Knowing how these things are taken apart and put together may help you become better at your craft.

Toward Forecasting

While my main practice of tarot for divination has been to learn more about myself and gain clarity for my choices, there is an element of excitement when one thinks about using these tools for seeing into the future. Especially when times are fraught, when there is a lot of uncertainty in the world and one is not sure what to do, it is easy to gain comfort from knowing a bit of the unknown. Our brains are prediction entities. Every step we take and every move we make is part of a game of anticipation and expectation. We are constantly plotting how things will move or how things will react as we interact with the world around us. And this helps us navigate the world. Our brain predicts and then learns from what happens—and then we course correct so that the next time we can predict with more accuracy. While most of this anticipation-prediction is done on a time scale for the next few milliseconds, seconds, or minutes, we also predict more distant events like weather or life events that allow us to plan ahead.

We don't know if nonhuman animals have the capacity to mind time travel like us, wandering into the future or into the past. There are some exciting new findings in the field of neuroforecasting that allude that our brain waves can unconsciously predict how things will transpire six months to even two years from now. Our individual choices can be detected in areas like the nucleus accumbens (positive choices) and the insula and amygdala (avoidance choices). We weigh the values of these choices in the prefrontal cortex. So, a lot of these decisions and ideas for the future are actually decided in our deep unconscious, and we may not even be aware that we have made that particular choice until much later. It would be lovely to see this being applied to ideas like divination.

Your Magical Divine Brain

As diviners who are tapping into the depths of our subconscious, I thought it would be amazing to learn more about how we do what we do. This is not essential for our practice, but it may help us understand how things work, make sense of things, and perhaps even become better at our craft. As diviners, we are also inherently curious and are seekers of knowledge, and what better way to explore than looking within ourselves?

I hope you found in this book a resource, a guide, and a personal journal to help you delve into your mind and expand your horizons. Your brain is glorious, magical, and divine. Dive in!

THANKS TO

Appa and Amma, Naren and Sowmiya, Harshita and Maanya. This couldn't have happened without you. We sat packing boxes, designing posters, and inviting folks to the first Neuro Tarot launch. Even though you didn't know what it all meant, you leaped in. And now we have a book.

Soumya (Sam), my sister, gossip mate, and confidante, for getting me my first tarot deck and perhaps giving me my first reading. Thanks for taking the time to tear some of this manuscript apart. It has become a better read because of you.

Victoria Vesna, for getting me to see the light of Art + Science and leading me out of basements of experiments. I have grown as a person and embraced my mystical side because of your open courage to explore everything. Goms, for constantly checking in, every day, for years.

Yuval and Sivan, for putting up with stressed and grumpy Appa while he muddled his way through the manuscript. And just being there. Thanks. Yuval still wonders at tarot and what crazy new thing I will propose next. And then he lets me dive into the crazy. Sivan, at three now, says, "Go finish your tarot book, Appa," and plays with the tarot decks I have hauled back from conferences. Who knows what she is learning, but it sure will be interesting.

My discovery of the tarot community was both a surprise and a welcome blessing. It was so welcoming and embraced me without inhibition. A big thanks to Michelle Welch for taking the chance on a scientist to come by NWTS in 2022. That broke open my doors to a whole new world of people and magic. Thanks for opening your world to me.

I met Barbara Moore also at the same conference, and stalked her a little bit. Thankfully she said she had also been looking for me. She held my hand through this process and has been such a positive light. To the team at Llewellyn, Marysa, Kat, and the amazing illustrators, thanks for making this book come alive. I also Facebook stalked Mat Auryn, and it just so happened he pinged me. (Psychic much?) I am so taken in by his generous spirit and encouragement.

Mary K. Greer, whom I sat next to at NWTS without knowing what to say, went out of her way to invite me to present with her at the Masters of Tarot Workshop at Omega in 2023. I learned so much in the process. Thank you, Mary, for writing such a beautiful foreword to this book.

Finally, to all of you who bought and enjoyed the Neuro Tarot deck, this book is a direct child of that endeavor. Your interest led me to explore more. This is for each of you.

Thank you!

GLOSSARY

affective empathy: ability to observe and mirror the physical reaction of the other to a situation or event

amygdala: part of the limbic system and the seat for fear and emotional processing

autonomic nervous system: controls a lot of automatic body responses such as eye dilation, lung expansion, etc.

basal ganglia: a region at the base of the forebrain responsible primarily for motor control, motor learning, executive functions and behaviors, and emotions

biorhythms: your internal body clocks based on diurnal cycles, arousal, and hormones

brain imaging: different techniques used to study the structure, function, and pharmacology of the brain, including functional magnetic resonance imaging (fMRI), positron-emission tomography (PET), diffusion tensor imaging (DTI), and so on; these kinds of techniques can be used to study normal brain functions and variations among individuals.

caudate nucleus: main integrator involved in intuitive processing

cognitive empathy: ability to understand the motivations, desires, and impulses that caused someone to behave a certain way

conceptualization: links perceptions of sensory input from the world with input from the body to create a meaningful psychological moment; conceptualization is the process by which stored representations of prior experiences (i.e., memories, knowledge) are used to make meaning out of sensations in the moment.

core affect: term used to describe the mental representation of bodily changes; core affect is usually accompanied by physical, kinesthetic, proprioceptive, and neurochemical fluctuations that take place within the core of the body and are represented in the brain.

default mode network: multiple areas in the brain that activate during reflections of self, ruminating, mind wandering, and mindful meditation

divination: in the context of this book, having extraordinary intuition or insight

emotional contagion: being affected by the emotions of others

empathy: the ability to understand and share the feelings of another

hypothalamus: controls a variety of body homeostasis mechanisms, such as hunger, satiety, and love; it also regulates hormones and immune function through the body, usually via the pituitary.

imagery/mental imagery/mind's eye: ability to visualize without any external sensory stimuli (quasi-perception)

insight: understanding the cause or logic behind a certain piece of knowledge; it is usually a sudden, conscious revelation.

insula: deep brain structure with representation of internal body structures

interoception: internal sensation of inner organs of the body

intuition: acquiring knowledge without any conscious notion, proof, logic, or evidence of that knowledge

locus coeruleus: area in the brain stem that is part of the "awareness" circuitry and thought to regulate your biorhythms; it releases the hormone / neurotransmitter norepinephrine.

medial prefrontal cortex: Part of the prefrontal cortex; activity in the MPFC can be used to understand how we perceive people spontaneously.

mentalizing: creating mental images of situations and outcomes of another person's behaviors and choices

mind wandering: free-flowing thoughts that are not constrained by the immediate context

mirroring: creating mental pictures or physical responses that mimic or mirror that observed in others

neuroforecasting: abilities of brain activity to predict events

neuroscience: study of the brain and the nervous system; while many immediately think just of the brain when they think of neuroscience, it is of importance to remember that we have neurons all through the body and that our hormonal and immune functions are also modulated by the nervous system, as well as our emotions and behavioral choices.

nucleus accumbens: mediates emotional and motivation processing, modulating reward and pleasure processing; it activates during positive behavior.

occipital lobe: situated in the rear of the skull; it is the smallest of the paired brain lobes and houses the visual centers.

orbitofrontal cortex: situated in the front of the brain (near the eye orbits); it serves as the location for current mental state of a person.

parietal lobe: integrates information from different sensory modalities and helps with spatial reasoning and attention

perception: brain processing that makes sense of what you see

positive affect/cognitive ease: the mental relief you get when you make an intuitive choice

prefrontal cortex: area controlling conscious processing, exerting control and inhibitions to actions; it adds values to actions.

querent/questioner: the person who is asking the question or stating the problem; in some cases, this may be the same person as the reader/diviner.

reader/diviner: the mystic who is using astrological charts, tarot cards, oracle cards, or some other tool to answer the questions at hand

retina: located in the back of the eye; the retina contains photoreceptors that convert light signals into electrical activity.

social cognition: the way in which people use information in social contexts to explain and predict their own behavior and that of others

superior marginal gyrus (SMG): the place in the brain that gets activated with a sense of "self"

superior temporal sulcus (STS): a groove in the temporal lobe that is implicated in mentalizing processes

temporal lobe: integrates visual and auditory information with long-term memory in the hippocampus

thalamus: termed as the relay center; it usually is a place where information comes in before being sent off to other parts of the brain. Think of a junction or a way station where a lot of exchange is happening.

umwelt: the world as perceived by an organism

visual center/V1: the primary visual cortex receives visual information and processes spatial mapping

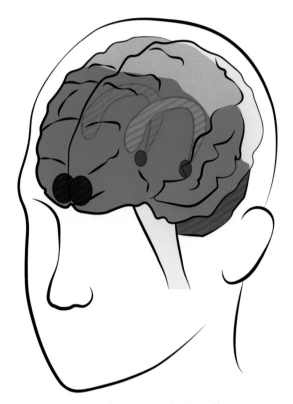

Illustration 13: Brain Doodles

BIBLIOGRAPHY

Arioli, Maria, Chiara Crespi, and Nicola Canessa. "Social Cognition through the Lens of Cognitive and Clinical Neuroscience." *Biomed Research International* (September 2018).

Barrett, Lisa Feldman, Batja Mesquita, Kevin N. Ochsner, and James J. Gross. "The Experience of Emotion." *Annu Review of Psychology* 58 (2007): 373–403.

Barrett, Lisa Feldman, and W. Kyle Simmons. "Interoceptive Predictions in the Brain." *Nature Reviews Neuroscience.* 16, no. 7 (July 2015): 419–29.

Bem, D. J. "Feeling the Future: Experimental Evidence for Anomalous Retroactive Influences on Cognition and Affect." *Journal of Personality and Social Psychology* 100, no. 3 (2011): 407–25.

Bubic, Andreja, D Yves von Cramon, and Richarda I Schubotz. "Prediction, Cognition and the Brain." *Frontiers in Human Neuroscience* 4, no. 25 (March 2010).

Carney, Dana R., Amy J. C. Cuddy, and Andy J. Yap. "Power Posing: Brief Nonverbal Displays Affect Neuroendocrine Levels and Risk Tolerance." *Psychological Science* 21, no. 10 (October 2010): 1363–8.

Christoff, Kalina, Caitlin Mills, Jessica R. Andrews-Hanna, Zachary C. Irving, Evan Thompson, Kieran C. R. Fox, and Julia W. Y. Kam. "Mind-Wandering as a Scientific Concept: Cutting through the Definitional Haze." *Trends in Cognitive Sciences* 22, no. 11 (November 2018): 95–959.

Dini, Hossein, Aline Simonetti, and Luis Emilio Bruni. "Exploring the Neural Processes behind Narrative Engagement: An EEG Study." *eNeuro* 10, no. 7 (July 2023): ENEURO.0484-22.2023.

Doherty, R. William. "The Emotional Contagion Scale: A Measure of Individual Differences." *Journal of Nonverbal Behavior* 21, no. 2 (1997): 131–54.

Garfinkel, Sarah N., Anil K. Seth, Adam B. Barrett, Keisuke Suzuki, and Hugo D. Critchley. "Knowing Your Own Heart: Distinguishing Interoceptive Accuracy from Interoceptive Awareness." *Biological Psychology* 104 (January 2015): 65–74.

Gilbert, Paul. "Compassion as a Social Mentality: An Evolutionary Approach." In *Compassion: Concepts, Research and Applications,* edited by Paul Gilbert, 31–68. London: Routledge, 2017.

Greenaway, Katharine H., Winnifred R. Louis, Matthew J. Hornsey. "Loss of Control Increases Belief in Precognition and Belief in Precognition Increases Control." *PLoS One* 8, no. 8 (August 2013): e71327.

Handler, Leonard, Ashley Campbell, and Betty Martin. "Use of Graphic Techniques in Personality Assessment: Reliability, Validity, and Clinical Utility." In *Comprehensive Handbook of Psychological Assessment* Vol. 2, *Personality Assessment*, edited by M. J. Hilsenroth and D. L. Segal, 387–404. Hoboken, NJ: John Wiley & Sons, 2004.

Horne, J. A., and Olov Ostberg. "A Self-Assessment Questionnaire to Determine Morningness Eveningness in Human Circadian Rhythms." *International Journal Chronobiology* 4, no. 2 (February 1976): 97–110.

Hruska, Pam, Kent G. Hecker, Sylvain Coderre, Kevin McLaughlin, Filomeno Cortese, Christopher Doig, Tanya Beran, Bruce Wright, and Olav Krigolson. "Hemispheric Activation Differences in Novice and Expert Clinicians during Clinical Decision Making." *Advances in Health Sciences Education* 21, no. 5 (December 2016): 921–33.

Gorvett, Zaria. "How the Menstrual Cycle Changes Women's Brains – For Better." *BBC*. August 6, 2018. https://www.bbc.com/future/article/20180806-how-the-menstrual-cycle-changes-womens-brains-every-month.

Jankowiak-Siuda, Kamila, Krystyna Rymarczyk, and Anna Grabowska. "How We Empathize with Others: A Neurobiological Perspective." *Medical Science Monitor* 17, no. 1 (January 2011): RA18–24.

Kitayama, Shinobu, and Cristina E. Salvador. "Culture Embrained: Going Beyond the Nature-Nurture Dichotomy." *Perspectives on Psychological Science.* 12, no. 5 (October 2017): 841–54.

Knutson, Brian, and Alexander Genevsky. "Neuroforecasting Aggregate Choice." *Current Directions in Psychol Science* 27, no. 2 (April 2018): 110–15.

Knutson, Brian, and Stephanie M. Greer. "Anticipatory Affect: Neural Correlates and Consequences for Choice." *Philosophical Transactions of the Royal Society B: Biological Sciences* 363, no. 1511 (December 2008): 3771–86.

Kober, Hedy, Lisa Feldman Barrett, Josh Joseph, Eliza Bliss-Moreau, Kristen Lindquist, and Tor D. Wager. "Functional Grouping and Cortical-Subcortical Interactions in Emotion: A Meta-Analysis of Neuroimaging Studies." *Neuroimage* 42, no. 2 (August 2008): 998–1031.

Konishi, Mahiko, Donald George McLaren, Haakon Engen, and Jonathan Smallwood. "Shaped by the Past: The Default Mode Network Supports Cognition that Is Independent of Immediate Perceptual Input." *PLoS One* 10, no. 6 (June 2015): e0132209.

Köster, Moritz, Shoji Itakura, Relindis Yovis, and Joscha Kärtner. "Visual Attention in 5-Year-Olds from Three Different Cultures." *PLoS One* 13, no. 7 (July 2018): e0200239.

Kragel, Philip A., and Kevin S. LaBar. "Decoding the Nature of Emotion in the Brain." *Trends in Cognitive Sciences* 20, no. 6 (June 2016):444–55.

Lindquist, Kristen A., Tor D. Wager, Hedy Kober, Eliza Bliss-Moreau, and Lisa Feldman Barrett. "The Brain Basis of Emotion: A Meta-Analytic Review." *Behavioral and Brain Sciences* 35, no. 3 (June 2012):121–43.

Maki, Pauline M., Jill B. Rich, and R. Shayna Rosenbaum. "Implicit Memory Varies across the Menstrual Cycle: Estrogen Effects in Young Women." *Neuropsychologia* 40, no. 5 (2002): 518–29.

Marks, David. "Visual Imagery Differences in the Recall of Pictures." *British Journal of Psychology* 64, no. 1 (March 1973): 17–24.

McCrea, Simon M. "Intuition, Insight, and the Right Hemisphere: Emergence of Higher Sociocognitive Functions." *Psychology Research Behavior Management* 3 (March 2010): 1–39.

Mehling, Wolf E., Michael Acree, Anita Stewart, Jonathan Silas, and Alexander Jones. "The Multidimensional Assessment of Interoceptive Awareness, Version 2 (MAIA-2)." *PLoS One* 13, no. 12 (December 2018): e0208034.

Nisbett, Richard E., and Takahiko Masuda. "Culture and Point of View." *Proceedings of the National Academy of Sciences of the United States of America* 100, no. 19 (September 2003): 11163–70.

Nummenmaa, Lauri, Enrico Glerean, Riitta Hari, and Jari K. Hietanen. "Bodily Maps of Emotions." *Proceedings of the National Academy of Sciences of the United States of America* 111, no. 2 (January 2014): 646–51.

Olenina, Ana Hedberg, Eric L. Amazeen, Bonnie Eckard, and Jason Papenfuss. "Embodied Cognition in Performance: The Impact of Michael Chekhov's Acting Exercises on Affect and Height Perception." *Frontiers in Psychology* 10 (October 2019): Article 2277.

Pearson, Joel, Thomas Naselaris, Emily A. Holmes, and Stephen M. Kosslyn. "Mental Imagery: Functional Mechanisms and Clinical Applications." *Trends in Cognitive Sciences* 19, no. 10 (October 2015): 590–602.

Riva, Federica, Chantal Triscoli, Claus Lamm, Andrea Carnaghi, and Giorgia Silani. "Emotional Egocentricity Bias Across the Life-Span." *Frontiers in Aging Neuroscience* 8 (April 2016): 74.

Salzman, C. Daniel, and Stefano Fusi. "Emotion, Cognition, and Mental State Representation in Amygdala and Prefrontal Cortex." *Annul Review of Neuroscience* 33 (July 2010): 173–202.

Sawhney and Khosla. "Where to Look for Insight" *Harvard Business Review,* November 2014. https://hbr.org/2014/11/where-to-look-for-insight.

Seth, Anil K., and Karl J. Friston. "Active Interoceptive Inference and the Emotional Brain." *Philosophical Transactions of the Royal Society B: Biological Sciences* 371 (November 2016).

Simony, Erez, Christopher J. Honey, Janice Chen, Olga Lositsky, Yaara Yeshurun, Ami Wiesel, and Uri Hasson. "Dynamic Reconfiguration of the Default Mode Network during Narrative Comprehension." *Nature Communications* 7 (July 2016): Article 12141.

Smallwood, Jonathan, and Jonathan W. Schooler. "The Science of Mind Wandering: Empirically Navigating the Stream of Consciousness." *Annual Review of Psychology* 66 (January 2015): 487–518.

Smith, Gabriel King, Caitlin Mills, Alexandra Paxton, and Kalina Christoff. "Mind-Wandering Rates Fluctuate across the Day: Evidence from an Experience-Sampling Study." *Cognitive Research: Principles and Implications* 3, no. 1 (December 2018): Article 54.

Song, Hayoung, Bo-yong Park, Hyunjin Park, and Won Mok Shim. "Cognitive and Neural State Dynamics of Narrative Comprehension." *Journal of Neuroscience* 41, no. 43 (October 2021): 8972–90.

Spunt, Robert P., and Ralph Adolphs. "The Neuroscience of Understanding the Emotions of Others." *Neuroscience Letters* 693 (February 2019): 44–48.

Tang, Yiyuan, Wutian Zhang, Kewei Chen, Shigang Feng, Ye Ji, Junxian Shen, Eric M. Reiman, and Yijun Liu. "Arithmetic Processing in the Brain Shaped by Cultures." *Proceedings of the National Academy of Sciences of the United States of America* 103, no. 28 (July 2006): 10775–80.

Taylor, Jon. "The Nature of Precognition." *Journal of Parapsychology* 78, no. 1 (2014): 19–38.

Tylén, K., P. Christensen, A. Roepstorff, T. Lund, S. Østergaard, and M. Donald. "Brains Striving for Coherence: Long-Term Cumulative Plot Formation in the Default Mode Network." *Neuroimage* 121 (November 2015): 106–14.

Walsh, Kevin S., Daivd P. McGovern, Andy Clark, and Redmond G. O'Connell. "Evaluating the Neurophysiological Evidence for Predictive Processing as a Model of Perception." *Annals of the New York Academy of Sciences* 1464, no. 1 (March 2020): 242–68.

Wan, Xiaohong, Daisuke Takano, Takeshi Asamizuya, Chisato Suzuki, Kenichi Ueno, Kang Cheng, Takeshi Ito, and Keiji Tanaka. "Developing Intuition:

Neural Correlates of Cognitive-Skill Learning in Caudate Nucleus." *Journal of Neuroscience* 32, no. 48 (November 2012): 17492–501.

Wang, Regina W. Y., Wei-Li Chang, Shang-Wen Chuang, and I-Ning Liu. "Posterior Cingulate Cortex Can Be a Regulatory Modulator of the Default Mode Network in Task-Negative State." *Scientific Reports* 9, no. 1 (May 2019): Article 7565.

Zander-Schellenberg, Thea, Carina Remmers, Johannes Zimmermann, Stefan Thommen, and Roselind Lieb. "It Was Intuitive, and It Felt Good: A Daily Diary Study on How People Feel When Making Decisions." *Cognition and Emotion* 33, no. 7 (November 2019): 1505–13.

Zanesco, Anthony P., Ekaterina Denkova, Joanna E. Witkin, and Amishi P. Jha. "Experience Sampling of the Degree of Mind Wandering Distinguishes Hidden Attentional States." *Cognition* 205 (December 2020):104380.

INDEX

NOTES

To Write to the Author

If you wish to contact the author or would like more information about this book, please write to the author in care of Llewellyn Worldwide Ltd. and we will forward your request. Both the author and publisher appreciate hearing from you and learning of your enjoyment of this book and how it has helped you. Llewellyn Worldwide Ltd. cannot guarantee that every letter written to the author can be answered, but all will be forwarded. Please write to:

Siddharth Ramakrishnan, PhD
℅ Llewellyn Worldwide
2143 Wooddale Drive
Woodbury, MN 55125-2989

Please enclose a self-addressed stamped envelope for reply,
or $1.00 to cover costs. If outside the U.S.A., enclose
an international postal reply coupon.

Many of Llewellyn's authors have websites with additional information and resources. For more information, please visit our website at http://www .llewellyn.com.